DR. CHRISTINE M. HUBBARD

AWAKENED
IDENTITY
NO LONGER A CAPTIVE

Published By: TamikaINK

Library of Congress Cataloging-in-Publication Data has been applied for
ISBN: 979-8-9881046-9-8
PRINTED IN THE UNITED STATES OF AMERICA

Table of Contents

Preface

I have invited the Holy Spirit to use this captivating book to awaken your inner man to your identity in Christ in a fresh way. May this spiritual journey of renewal in the knowledge of God in Christ demolish strongholds of darkness, break any shackles and weight of unbelief in your heart, and advance you into the revival of the freedom God provides you in Christ.

God has reconciled us to Himself in His infinite love by forming a group of believers in devotion to serving him in spirit and truth. Within each believer, the sacred presence of the Holy Spirit is a divine impartation that connects our hearts with the image and likeness of God in Christ.

Now, firmly anchored in the body of Christ, we stand unwavering, embracing the liberty that is our birthright. However, among many lies a yoke of enslavement, a snare that entangles those unaware of the freedom found in Christ. Let us examine ourselves to see if some areas need sanctification unto God.

Countless souls remain entangled in the intricate web of darkness, caught in lies woven by the enemy. However, through Christ, we possess dominion over any belief system that opposes the knowledge of

God. We are seated in the heavenly realms, accepted, made righteous heirs of God, and joint heirs with Christ.

Let the following chapters resonate deeply within your being, stirring your spirit and illuminating the journey ahead. Additionally, may the wisdom and profound truths in this book ignite a flame within your soul, awakening your divine purpose in Christ.

As children of God, let us embark on this sacred quest, guided by the Holy Spirit, as we uncover our glorious life in Christ that transcends the limitations of our past while offering endless possibilities for our present and future life in Christ.

Break free from the shackles of an unproductive mindset, renewing your mind with thoughts that elevate your God-consciousness. Discover a higher realm of studies that embrace and celebrate your God-given identity in Christ. Together, let us venture forth, embracing our freedom in Christ. Prepare for a life-changing renewal and spiritual growth as you read: "AWAKENED IDENTITY NO LONGER A CAPTIVE."

Prayer

Heavenly Father, in Jesus' name, I invite the Holy Spirit to use the inspiration in this captivating book to touch the depths of the reader's soul with renewal and restoration to awaken their identity in Christ. May any shackles binding their heart be shattered, granting them the freedom found in Christ. Let these words ignite a transformative journey, breaking the chains of bondage and awakening their divine purpose. As they delve into this book, may their mind be renewed and their identity in Christ embraced.

Holy Father, thank you for the glorious opportunity to write and express the gift of grace upon me abounding in knowledge and fruitful vintage of increase watering the reader's soul. May a wave of eternal glory illuminate the beautiful resources available daily in Christ while reading this book in the name of Jesus. Amen.

Part 1: Foundational Concepts and Mind Transformation

Chapter One:
The Process of Becoming New in Christ

Scripture: Galatians 2:20, John 1:12, Romans 5

In the journey of becoming new in Christ, we daily embrace a transformative process reflecting God's power in our lives. In Galatians 2:20, Paul presents this powerful truth: "I am crucified with Christ: nevertheless, I live; yet not I, but Christ liveth in me: and the life which I now live in the flesh I live by the faith of the Son of God who loved me and gave himself for me." Through faith in the Son of God, who loved us and gave Himself for us, we experience a profound exchange of our old selves for the indwelling presence of Christ.

John 1:12 reminds us that as we receive Jesus and believe in His name, we are granted the power to become sons and daughters of God. This incredible privilege stems from God's vision of shedding His love abroad in our hearts through the Holy Spirit. He approves and accepts us, calling us to manifest a kingly and priestly character with authority.

"Become" is a powerful word that signifies the spoken word over our lives, manifesting its reality as we receive it into our hearts. By applying faith, continually confessing, and applying our sonship, we activate the full potential of becoming children of God. Submission to God's will enables us to reach the heights of our sonship and make the scriptural narrative a tangible reality.

Our new life in Christ is a continual process of growth and transformation. It is essential to grasp the significance of our identity and purpose in Him. Genesis 1:26 reveals that we are made in God's image and likeness, intending to fellowship with Him. However, through the fall of Adam, sin entered the world, leading to spiritual separation and a loss of glory.

Yet, we find restoration and reconciliation in the last Adam, Jesus Christ. Through Him, we are born anew, empowered to walk in the fullness of our identity as sons and daughters of God and called to cultivate our souls, prospering in the likeness of Christ, who is our wisdom, righteousness, sanctification, and redemption.

As we align our mind with the mind of Christ, our character exemplifies transformation. We recognize that our old identity has changed, and we now bear the image of Christ. No longer are we defined by our past or the opinions of others. In Christ, we are complete and accepted by God, possessing the power to condemn every voice that tries to diminish our identity.

The process of becoming new in Christ involves growth and development. We are His workmanship, created in Christ Jesus unto good works. By aligning ourselves with God's perspective and living according to His will, we bring meaning and substance to our lives. The Holy Spirit witnesses this transformation within us, testifying to the new covenant in which God writes his laws on the table of our hearts, and He remembers our sins are no longer.

Separating ourselves from the world and touching not the unclean things is part of our calling, which applies to God's will for our separation. In doing so, our heavenly Father becomes a loving and nurturing presence in our lives. We become His sons and daughters, manifesting His glory and righteousness. This growth is essential for us to develop the newness of Christ within us.

Therefore, let us lay aside every weight and sin that hinders us, running the race before us with patience and endurance. Let us draw inspiration from the cloud of witnesses who have gone before us, testifying to the transformative power of Christ. As we grow and mature in our new identity, we mirror His image and carry out His purpose in the world.

A Personal Testimony: Illuminated and Infused with Spiritual Significance:

In this profound testimony, I invite you to witness one of the many awe-inspiring stories of God's magnificent grace in my life as He worked miraculously to transform me into a new creation in Christ. It revolves around the pivotal moment when I heeded the call to awaken to a new life and break free from the clutches of sin's captivity, forever altering the course of my existence.

One day, I sat down to write a letter to sever the ties with the airman I was in a relationship with. The Holy Spirit's gentle voice guided me through a series of soul-searching questions as I began writing the letter. I grappled with the first question in the depths of my being when he asked: "What is a man that I should lose my soul?" With heartfelt conviction, I responded, "Nothing, Lord." The Spirit's probing continued, asking, "What are some sufferings now for my namesake compared to the joy I have for you?" And again, my resolute answer echoed, "Nothing, Lord."

Through composing that "dear John" letter, I discovered a newfound strength surging within me. With each word penned, I relinquished the bondage of that ungodly relationship, and an overwhelming assurance of peace flooded my soul—God had delivered me from the darkness of that sinful lifestyle. Indeed, I awakened to my new identity in Christ. I emerged from captivity, embracing my newfound identity in Christ, ready to walk in unbroken fellowship with the Lord.

Even though my airmen friend had entrusted me with his car and power of attorney, granting me access to all his material possessions and resources, I willingly surrendered it all to follow the Lord on my journey of transformation wholeheartedly. Before he returned from overseas, I packed his car full of the gifts and things he had given me and parked it at my parent's house. I gave him back everything he had left with me and had given to me, indicating my liberation from the chains that once bound me. I was no longer a captive of that ungodly relationship—now awakened to newness in Christ.

As I continued this radical and positive change in my outlook on life's transformative path in Christ, I settled on a journey of renewing my mind and understanding the true essence of following the Lord. I immersed myself in the teachings of Matthew 10:38, where Jesus declared, "And he that taketh not his cross, and followeth after me, is not worthy of me." This profound truth reshaped my priorities as I realized the significance of embracing the level of ministry that comes with answering the call of obedience to walk with the Lord. It is challenging to find words describing how transformative and enriching it became to study the word of God. Psalm 119 verse 162 describes my spirit's state: "I rejoice at thy word, as one that findeth great spoil." In this place of conversion, I found the treasure of a life filled with purpose, peace, and prosperity.

Moreover, Jesus's words in Matthew 10:37 resonated deeply within me: "He that loveth father or mother more than me is not worthy of me: and he that loveth son or daughter more than me is not worthy of me." As I accepted these divine instructions, my life's canvas changed into a masterpiece of godliness, exhibiting the shining image of a woman reborn in Christ.

Being awakened to this captivating journey showcases the magnificent power of grace and the profound impact of obedience to God's call. As you read my story, it beckons you to embark on your quest for liberation, inspiring you to embrace this unique path of spiritual renewal and prioritize your relationship with Christ above all else.

In conclusion, becoming new in Christ is a journey of a call to greatness and restoration. It involves embracing our identity as sons and daughters of God, aligning our minds with the mind of Christ, and growing in the knowledge of His love and grace. Through faith and continuous surrender to His will, we experience the fullness of His glory, shining as lights in this present dark world. I came awakened to my identity in Christ.

Prayer

Mighty and Holy Father, I humbly approach Your glorious presence, enveloped in the precious Name of Jesus, with a heart overflowing with gratitude. Through Your boundless grace, You have bestowed upon me the immeasurable gift of life in Christ. I stand in awe as You, the Creator of all things, have chosen me to be Your beloved child, fashioned in Your image and likeness. No living thing on this earth can compare to the divine purpose You have instilled within me. Thank you for making me alive in Christ.

The profound revelation of Your Word illuminates my understanding, unveiling the depths of Your character as both God and the Father of my faith. In Your divine Sovereignty, You encompass every aspect of my existence. You are my unwavering provider, ensuring every need I may experience; you are my unfailing protector, shielding me from harm and my faithful healer, restoring and renewing my spirit. Your constant outpouring of love and favor sustains me, enabling me to flourish and thrive in the depths of my being.

You fortify my innermost being with faith, granting me unwavering stability and profound soundness. Through this steadfast faith, I trust entirely You, surrendering every aspect of my heart, mind, and soul. As the Father of my faith, You have lavished an incomparable love upon me, embracing and uniting me with the glorious person of Christ. In Him, I find my identity and purpose intricately woven into the fabric of your divine plan.

In the majestic presence of Christ in me, elevation to heavenly places seated with him is a seat of honor. In this exalted position, I inherit a royal residence of adoption, clothed with authority and power. With the very breath of heaven, I declare Your divine will upon this Earth. Your wisdom and dominion flow through me, impacting lives and transforming the world through your grace imparted unto me.

In the all-encompassing and matchless Name of Jesus, I seal this prayer, acknowledging Him as my Savior and Lord. Through His precious sacrifice, I can stand before You, Holy Father, and experience the fullness of Your glory. As I utter this resounding "Amen," may the spiritual impact of this prayer echo throughout my life, unleashing a divine anointing that transcends time and space. In Jesus' name, I pray. Amen

Chapter Two:
The Mind of Christ

T he "Mind of Christ" concept is uplifting and transformative for believers. It refers to the ability to think, perceive, and comprehend things from the perspective of Jesus Christ. As followers of Christ, we are encouraged to have the mind of Christ, which means aligning our thoughts, attitudes, and actions with His illustrations and teachings.

In 1 Corinthians 2:16, the verse emphasizes that no one can fully comprehend the mind of the Lord or instruct Him, but as believers, we have the mind of Christ. Having the mind of Christ implies that we can access His wisdom, understanding, and divine perspective through our relationship with Him.

Philippians 2:5-8 provides a deeper insight into the mind of Christ. It describes Jesus' humility and selflessness, as He willingly took the form of a servant and humbled Himself, even to death on the cross. As believers, we are encouraged to let this same mind be in us, following Jesus' example of humility, sacrifice, and obedience.

Philippians 3:15 highlights the importance of having the mind of Christ as a mindset for believers. It urges us to pursue spiritual maturity and unity in the faith, seeking to align our thoughts and attitudes with the knowledge of the Son of God. This attitude of pursuing spiritual maturity implies that our growth and transformation as believers involve adopting the mind of Christ and allowing God to reveal His truth to us.

The process of developing the mind of Christ is a spiritual journey that involves spiritual warfare. According to 2 Corinthians 10:4-5, our weapons are not carnal but mighty through God for pulling down strongholds. Through the power of God, we cast down imaginations and every thought that exalts itself against the knowledge of God, bringing every thought into captivity to the obedience of Christ. This process emphasizes the importance of actively renewing our minds and rejecting thoughts and ideas contradicting God's truth.

Having the mind of Christ requires a deliberate choice to pray and align our thinking with His. It involves renewing our minds through prayer, studying and meditating on God's Word, and fellowship with the Holy Spirit. We resist the influence of worldly thinking and embrace the thoughts and values of Christ.

Ultimately, having the mind of Christ leads to a transformation of our character and actions. It empowers us to live according to God's will, love others selflessly, and make choices that honor Him. As we grow in the mind of Christ, we begin to understand our identity as new creatures in Him, partakers of His righteousness, and heirs of His promises.

Understanding the power of prayer plays a vital role in developing the mind of Christ. We invite His presence and guidance by communing with God and surrendering our thoughts and desires to Him. We acknowledge Him as our provider, protector, and healer, and we rely on His grace and favor to sustain us. Through prayer, we express our gratitude and dependence on God, seeking His wisdom and seeking to align our will with His.

In conclusion, the mind of Christ is a powerful spiritual concept that encourages believers to think, perceive, and act in alignment with Jesus Christ. It involves humility, sacrifice, obedience, and a deliberate choice to renew our minds and align our thoughts with God's truth. By developing the mind of Christ, we transform and empower our life of faith to reflect His love and grace to the world.

Prayer of Faith

Heavenly Father, I come before You with gratitude and awe for your transformative work in Christ for me. I thank You for making me alive unto You, calling me into Your family, and equipping me to fulfill Your purposes.

Lord, being awakened to my identity in Christ, I embrace the reality that just beneath the surface of my thought life is the living witness of the Holy Spirit to guide me into all truth. I surrender to His calling, inviting Him to awaken the treasure of Christ within me so that I may live in alignment with your ordained plans for my life in Christ.

Holy Spirit, I invite You to stir the deep places within me, awakening me to the abundant life You have prepared for me in Christ. Help me to fully comprehend and embrace the reality of being born into Your family as a lively stone, in a holy and royal priesthood. May I shine forth Your praises and fulfill Your purpose in Christ.

I acknowledge that I am no longer captive to outward appearances or the expectations of others. Through accepting Jesus Christ as my Savior, I am born into Your family, called to be a lively stone in Your spiritual house and part of a holy and royal priesthood to show forth Your praises and live for Your glory and purpose.

Having the mind of Christ equips me to make a deliberate choice to pray and align my thinking with His. I recognize I am part of the pillar and ground of truth in the Church of the living God. By the power of Jesus' resurrection, I am alive unto You. I deeply desire to embrace this reality and fellowship with You deeper, partaking more freely of my daily inheritance in Christ.

Help me worship You in spirit and truth, fully embracing all You have fulfilled for me through Christ. Enable me to live in the exalted position of being alive unto You, accessing the riches of Your glory, and making Your riches in Christ known to the world around me. The process of developing the mind of Christ is a spiritual journey that involves spiritual warfare.

Lord, I understand I have authority over the enemy and his devices. I commit to walking in the delegated authority entrusted to me, faithfully seeking You each day. I desire to diligently pursue Your presence, knowing that You are a rewarder of those who diligently seek You.

I surrender all areas of my life to You that have kept me captive. I choose to walk by faith and not by sight, trusting Your word and relying on Your guidance.

I submit to Your thoughts and ways, allowing Your truth to expose any falsehood within me.

Lord, I long to become a living witness, just like the Samaritan woman whose encounter with Jesus transformed her life. May my life be an open letter reflecting the heart of Christ within me. I declare that I am no longer confined to darkness or prejudice but constantly alive unto You with purpose and vision.

As I rewrite the next chapter of my life, I take a firm stance against an impoverished mentality that accepts things as they are. I decree my freedom in Christ and embrace my identity. I agree with Your will, Lord, protecting my spirit and guarding against the enemy's invasion. As a follower of Christ, I am encouraged to have the mind of Christ, which means aligning my thoughts, attitudes, and actions with your teachings and examples.

I am alive unto You, O God, and I desire to bring glory to Your name. May my life testify to Your grace, love, and power. Guide me as I walk this journey, continually drawing closer to You and fulfilling the plans You have for me.

In the mighty name of Jesus, I pray. Amen.

Chapter Three: Transforming Our Thought Life: Embracing Spiritual Impact

Our Thought Life Matters: Unlocking the Power Within

In the hustle and bustle of life, our thoughts often go unnoticed. Yet, they possess a profound spiritual significance that shapes our existence. Irrespective of our backgrounds, all humans have a mind capable of imagination, will, emotion, and thought. Our thoughts can lead us to bondage, oppression, and depression or guide us toward health, wealth, and peace. Adversity and temptation are inevitable aspects of human experience, as affirmed in 1 Corinthians 10:13. However, our thoughts hold the key to our growth and behavior, making cultivating a fruitful thought life crucial.

The Foundation of Our Thought Life: The Culture of Words and Childhood Conditioning

Our thought life finds its roots in the words and conditioning we receive during childhood. If we find ourselves trapped in negative thought patterns from our upbringing, escaping that fortress of negative thoughts requires upgrading our thinking. Mentally reshaping our thought life requires seeing through the lens of the knowledge of God found in the Scriptures. Apostle Paul aptly states in 1 Corinthians 13:11, "When I was a child, I spake as a child, I understood as a child, I thought as a child: but when I became a man, I put away childish things." This scripture emphasizes the impact of thoughts on our personal growth as we mature. Our thoughts lay the foundation for decision-making, which ultimately shapes the outcomes we experience in life. Therefore, developing and aligning our spirit with truth from the Word of God is essential to our thought life.

Guarding the Heart: The Source of Life's Manifestations

Proverbs 4:23 instructs us to diligently guard our hearts, for the issues of life flow out of it. Our heart, the seat of our emotions and desires, is deeply interconnected with our thought life. Nurturing our hearts through the wisdom of God's Word sustains our spirits, as highlighted in Proverbs 18:14. Understanding the power of our thoughts is crucial in our decision-making. When we use God's knowledge, it empowers us to choose thoughts aligned with God's truth. Apostle Paul admonishes us in Philippians 4:8 to think about things that are honest, true, lovely, just, and of a good report.

The Battlefield of the Mind: Casting Down Imagination and Bringing Thoughts into Captivity

In 2 Corinthians 10:5, we see that we are to cast down imaginations and every high thing that exalts itself against the knowledge of God. This scripture calls us to bring every thought into captivity to the obedience of Christ. Our thoughts establish patterns that shape our decisions, ultimately influencing the outcomes we experience. Through developing our spirit to align and capture thoughts with truth, we can capture thoughts that would otherwise create barriers to thinking with the mind of Christ.

The Power of Kingly Thinking and Speaking: Words, Images, and Identity

The words we speak have immense power and influence in our lives. Just as a king's words carry authority and power, as stated in Ecclesiastes 8:4, our speech should reflect a kingly fashion, seeing we are kings and priests unto God. Ecclesiastes 8:4 reminds us of the power present in the expressions of a king. We access God's Kingdom of Light by choosing our words and identifying with our appointed place of kings and priests as God has set us. We are insightful-speaking spirits walking as kings and priests unto God. Recognizing this truth allows us to align our thinking and speaking with our true identity in Christ. Think and talk like an heir in the kingdom of God.

Unveiling the Canvas of Life: Thoughts, Ink, and the Power of Thinking

Our thoughts play a significant role in shaping the canvas of our lives. Proverbs 23:7 affirms that as a man thinks in his heart, so is he. Our thinking ability is a powerful gift from our Creator. As we think, we live. Understanding this truth, we believe, like kings, taking charge of having our seats in the Kingdom, reigning and guarding our minds and choices. Our thoughts serve as portals through which we receive and enter the activities of human life.

Strength and Insulation in Thin Thinking: Resisting Captivity and Faintness in Adversity

Thin thinking, lacking the strength to withstand adversities, can leave us vulnerable and unstable. Proverbs 24:10 warns that our strength is small if we faint in the day of adversity. When we think right, we strengthen and insulate our spirits to stand firm even amidst the storms of life. Developing a solid thought life allows us to overcome challenges empowered by God's Word.

A Personal Testimony: The Unveiling of Knowledge

Prepare to be spiritually captivated as I share my journey within the pages of this chapter, where the transformative power of God's grace shines brilliantly. Join me as I recount a series of extraordinary moments that led to my emancipation from the shackles of captivity and its profound impact on my identity in Christ.

My story begins on a humble farm, where I grew up alongside my parents and siblings. There, amidst the simplicity of rural life, I witnessed a pivotal event. On a fateful day, our tranquil existence on the porch, shelling peas, was disrupted by the arrival of an angry landowner who directed derogatory words toward my father. My mother's unwavering faith sprang forth in that crucial moment as she fearlessly challenged the discriminatory remarks made in front of her children to her husband. Our mother jumped up, spilling her pan of peas, and confronted the landowner, compelling her to retreat in haste. This unforgettable scene, etched in my memory, illustrated the power of boldness in speaking out against discriminatory responses that sought to diminish our worth as children growing up on a farm.

The impact of that incident reverberated within me, igniting a fire of courage and self-worth. It became clear to me that God expects us to stand firm in the image of Christ, unyielding to those who would assert superiority over us. My mother's unwavering stance against prejudice left an indelible mark, inspiring me to recognize the potential consequences of labeling individuals based on the color of their skin. I resolved never to accept a false identity imposed by others but to embrace the truth of who God had uniquely created me to be in my skin color.

As we relocated to a new farm, fresh challenges awaited me. At the age of sixteen, I stumbled upon gross inaccuracies in the calculations submitted by our new landowner regarding my father's rightful share of the harvest. Driven by a deep sense of justice, I immersed myself in unraveling the truth, seeking proof to confront the landlord. Armed with meticulously calculated figures, I unveiled the landlord's deception, exposing the unjust treatment inflicted upon us. In anger, the landlord retaliated by cutting down his apple trees, symbols of sustenance and provision for us. Eventually, he demanded that my daddy leave his property, fearing that the intelligence and resilience the

Lord had given me were intermeddling with his dishonesty.

These experiences propelled me into a lifelong mission to advocate for those without a voice to champion justice for the marginalized. The influence of my father's upbringing, shaped by the lingering remnants of a slavery mentality, had limited his ability to comprehend the true worth he deserved. His mother, my grandmother, taught him to believe his race was inferior to the man he was farming with. This experience caused me to understand the influence of one's beliefs about race, which underscores the generational impact such attitudes can have on your mind. This powerful and personal mission to advocate for justice and the marginalized shaped my thought life significantly. Advocating for those without a voice and championing justice for the marginalized became a noble endeavor. My family history of being marginalized has provided me with a unique perspective and motivation to work toward positive change.

It became increasingly evident that my thoughts and beliefs could shape my destiny, and I was determined to break free from the chains of inferiority that had gripped my daddy and his mother. Their mentality crippled them into believing a lie, thus hindering their success to become all that God had ordained for them. At a young age, gaining insight into the meaning of words became an early pursuit, with the dictionary serving as my guide in unraveling their significance.

Many years later, I turned to the Word of God, seeking wisdom and revelation as to why I was trained to feel inferior based on my skin tone. Through this spiritual exploration, I discovered that my skin color held no bearing on my ability to achieve equality and fulfillment. The grace of God illuminated my true identity, releasing me from the bondage of wrong thinking and empowering me to emerge as a woman of purpose and strength.

Unveiling the Truth: Perception of Identity

I want to share another profound revelation that transformed my perception of identity. Join me as I recount a pivotal moment during my luncheon hour, where the truth of my true self emerged, guided by the prompting of the Holy Spirit.

No longer bound by the need for external affirmation, I realized that my Creator had set me free from the chains of distorted thinking. I entered a realm where God reigns as Lord and King over my thoughts, banishing emotional bondage and embracing the truth of His unconditional love. In a transformative moment during a quiet lunch, the Holy Spirit unveiled the profound truth behind my identity. He stripped the letter "k" from the word "skin," exposing the issue of wrong thinking rooted in our sinful nature. A paradigm shift forever altered my perspective, redirecting my focus from external appearances to the depth of our shared humanity.

Raised in an environment that instilled feelings of inferiority based on skin tone differences, I grappled with a sense of otherness shaped by prejudiced beliefs. However, everything changed when the Holy Spirit urged me to look with understanding, peeling away the layers of societal conditioning. In that sacred moment, I realized that my self-perception should not be determined by how others viewed me but by how my Creator saw me.

Examining my life at different stages, I often felt inadequately qualified compared to others. Yet, the Holy Spirit continued to prompt me, inviting me to explore more profound truths. He led me to remove the letter "k" from the word "skin," exposing the core issue: "sin." It was a profound turning point that shifted my perspective. I understood that the fundamental problem lay not in our external appearances but in our shared fallen nature as human beings.

Delving even further, the Holy Spirit unveiled a remarkable revelation. By removing the letter "s" from the word "skin," I discovered that we are all "kin" born in sin, bound by a common struggle. This revelation shattered the illusion of superiority and inferiority, dismantling the faulty mindset that had hindered my true freedom.

Christ's wisdom brushed against my knowledge in that transformative moment, reshaping my thought life as I continued on my lunch hour sitting across from a woman of a different skin tone; the imprint of Christ upon my mind continued to captivate me. He asked me a question by saying: "What is the difference between you and the woman you are facing?" The Holy Spirit guided me deeper into deliverance by posing another profound question: "What color is faith?" In a powerful and impactful manner, the Holy Spirit unveiled that faith transcends color because it is rooted in power. He taught me to see myself by faith, not by the color of my skin. This revelation continues to resonate within me, empowering me to boldly live above any form of discrimination, secure in the knowledge that my faith grants me the power to overcome and flourish.

Now, I confidently embrace my God-given identity, no longer bound by the damage of sin or societal barriers. I stand among those who have chosen to live anew in Christ daily, liberated from the shackles of a sinful mindset. My faith propels me to soar above the limitations that prejudice may seek to impose, for in the realm of God's truth; there is no room for skin color to divide. I revel in the freedom to live authentically in my God-given skin, rejoicing in the transformative power of Christ's wisdom and the liberation it brings.

Transforming Identity and Overcoming Discrimination: Skin, Sin, and Kinship

Discrimination based on skin color can leave deep scars on our thought lives. However, understanding the actual root issue transforms our perspective. Removing the "k" from "skin" reveals the word "sin." We are all "kin" in sin, born into a fallen world. Our faith, which transcends color, holds the power to live above discrimination and societal barriers. By embracing our God-given identity, we can rise above the damage caused by sin and experience the freedom to live confidently in our skin.

Conclusion: Reclaiming Our Thought Life: Embracing the Mind of Christ

Our thought life holds immense spiritual significance, impacting every aspect of our existence. We can break free from mental captivity and experience transformation by aligning our thoughts with God's truth. Cultivating a thought life rooted in the mind of Christ empowers us to overcome adversity, resist negative influences, and embrace our identity. Let us embark on this journey of renewing our minds, recognizing the power of our thoughts, and embracing the spiritual impact that comes from aligning our thinking with the wisdom of God's Word.

Prayer

Almighty and Merciful Father, in Jesus' name, I humbly bow before Your throne, overwhelmed by Your grace and compassion that shines through when my soul is ignorant of Your power to defend and make me whole again. In the depths of my pain and sorrow, You remain steadfast, a Father who understands and empathizes with my every struggle. I am grateful you symbolize goodness, an unwavering pillar of support in my life.

Oh Lord, You are the wellspring of wisdom, knowledge, and understanding. I surrender my limited experience to Your divine guidance, knowing You possess infinite wisdom beyond my comprehension. I find solace in the vastness of Your grace, for it is through Your boundless love that every need in Christ Jesus, according to the riches of Your glory, is abundantly supplied,

I thank You, Heavenly Father, for uncovering the trapping of prejudices that confront our lives from time to time. I know You have cleared my mind to think above words that exalt themselves against Your knowledge of making all men equal. In You, Holy Father, all men live and have their being; all life springs from You. I am thankful to be alive in You without fear or intimidation.

I declare Your name with reverence and awe as I conclude this prayer. In the precious and powerful name of Jesus, I seal this prayer, acknowledging that I find refuge, strength, and hope in You. May Your Spirit continue to move within me, transforming my life and illuminating the path ahead. In Jesus' name, I pray, Amen.

Part 2: Identifying and Overcoming Challenges

DR. CHRISTINE M. HUBBARD

Chapter Four:
The Inevitable Breeding Ground for Captivity

—————————◆❀◆—————————

In Deuteronomy 32:18, Jeremiah 2:11, Isaiah 1:3, Jeremiah 2:32, and Psalm 78:10-11, we are confronted with the sobering reality of God's people forgetting Him and forsaking His ways. These verses depict a state of captivity, where the breeding ground for negative relationships and conditions gets established. The word "inevitable" emphasizes that if this situation is not corrected, the consequences of captivity are inescapable.

We see the initial instance of this breeding ground for captivity in the story of Adam and Eve in the Garden of Eden. Through their acceptance of deceptive knowledge that exalted itself against God's wisdom, they fell into captivity, falling short of God's glory. They recognized their nakedness and attempted to cover their shame with fig leaves. However, it was only through encountering a covering of God's grace prevailed to protect them. In the same way, when we meet God through His grace, He covers our sins and removes our shame, liberating us from the captivity of sin.

The term "breeding ground" refers to an environment suitable for fostering the development of an idea. Initially, Adam and Eve were in the perfect breeding ground of Eden, where the presence of God fulfilled them daily. It was an environment perfectly designed to cultivate and nurture their relationship with their Creator. In this unspoiled home, free of corruption, they had unbroken fellowship with God, who provided everything they needed. However, when they turned away from God, they entered a different breeding ground where sin abounded and led to inevitable captivity. The Scriptures attest to the downward spiral of humanity's sinfulness and the consequences it brought.

Throughout the Old and New Testaments, we find accounts of captives in emotional webs of activities and bondages, individuals, and even nations who have forgotten God. Deuteronomy 32:18 describes a people unmindful of the Rock who begat them, while Jeremiah 2:13 speaks of God's people forsaking Him, the fountain of living waters, and turning to broken cisterns. Their captivity resulted from disobedience, ignorance, deception, and false teachings. Lamentations 2:14 reveals how their prophets lacked the knowledge of God, contributing to the nation's captivity.

But as believers, we are called to cast down imaginations and every high thing that exalts itself against the knowledge of God, bringing every thought into captivity to the obedience of Christ (2 Corinthians 10:3-6). Ignorance of God's Word creates a breeding ground for captivity, but acknowledging this root cause can bring about a transformative revelation of peace through God's grace. By living in the light of truth, we no longer remain captive but are pre-empted by the transforming power of God's grace.

God has given us His Word, which cleanses and renews our minds, leading to freedom in our spirits. Romans 3:23 acknowledges that all have sinned and fallen short of God's glory. Through the mediation of Jesus Christ, glory has returned treasured in earthen vessels, making our bodies a spiritual habitation indwelt by God. By renewing our minds with the Scriptures and identifying with the mind of Christ, we experience freedom from captivity. The Word of God washes us clean, removes shame, and empowers us to walk in the newness of life.

In various biblical accounts, we witness how God releases captives from the bondage of sin, paying the price for our deliverance through Christ. As we receive His grace, we are set free from the residue of shame and failure. God desires us to walk in the promises of His Kingdom, leaving behind the captivity of our past.

The strength to break free from negative thinking and escape the chains of bondage rests in the knowledge of Christ. A single word from God can turn our situations around, as we possess the power to remove the bars of captivity through His instruction. By embracing the truth of God's Word and aligning our thoughts with His, we experience liberation from the breeding ground of captivity, finding freedom, and walking in the fullness of life that God has ordained for us in Christ.

Prayer

eavenly Father, in the precious name of Jesus, I humbly come before Your throne, recognizing the greatness of Your name and the immeasurable power that resides in You. I stand in awe of Your ability to restore and redeem my life, even in the face of failures and mistakes. You have created a haven of peace and love where I find solace and renewal.

Oh Lord, I discover a life that overflows with kindness and compassion in You. Your willingness to shape me into a vessel of honor astounds me. I am grateful, Holy Father, for your delight in establishing a daily connection with me through Your sustaining grace and boundless love. I am humbled by the privilege of experiencing Your divine presence, knowing that You guide and uphold me in everything.

Father, Your love envelops me, nourishing my spirit and empowering me to press forward. Your grace covers my shortcomings, offering me a fresh start each day. In this embrace of Your mercy, I find my worth and purpose. Walking in the hope of eternal fellowship with You is an honor.

In the matchless name of Jesus, I offer this prayer, knowing that You hear and answer the cries of

Your children. May Your name be glorified, honored, and respected in my life and all who call upon Your name, in Jesus' name. Amen.

Chapter Five:
The Consequences of
Rejecting Christ

H ebrews 12:25 urges us not to refuse the One who speaks, reminding us that if those who rejected Him on earth did not escape judgment, how much more severe will it be for us if we turn away from Him who speaks from heaven?

The rejection of Christ has significant implications for the soul of man. From the very foundation of the world, God established redemption through Christ, desiring to make man whole, complete, and united in Him, the Creator of all things.

In Ephesians 3:8, the apostle Paul shares that he has been entrusted with the grace to proclaim the unsearchable riches of Christ among the Gentiles. He aims to reveal the fellowship of the mystery hidden in God since the beginning of the world so all might know God's manifold wisdom through Jesus Christ.

Rejecting Christ leads to captivity and the judgment of God. As John 12:48 declares, those who reject Christ and refuse His words will face judgment on the last day, for His words will be the basis of that judgment.

Moreover, rejecting Christ distorts one's true identity before one's Maker. In Genesis 1:26, God declared His intention to create man in His image and likeness. Any knowledge that contradicts this truth should be rejected and cast down. We can find assurance in Colossians 1:27 that Christ in us is the hope of glory, and in Colossians 1:15, we learn that Christ is the image of the invisible God, fully embodying the Godhead. The magnificent flow of glory, majesty, and power from God to man through Christ is beyond man's comprehension!

Understanding our identity in Christ is crucial to breaking free from the captivity of deception and lies of the enemy. Christ's victory over the enemy is purposed for us to experience daily. Rejecting Him means denying God's intended victory for our lives, forfeiting the gift of righteousness, and denying the abundant life He offers.

Let us firmly establish that the Bible is the inspired Word of God, profitable for doctrine, reproof, correction, and instruction in righteousness (2 Timothy 3:16). It teaches us about Christ and His redemptive work, serving as the source of light and truth for our existence on Earth. Despite adverse claims or rejections, the Word of God remains valid, authentic, and sound. Man's dismissal of the proof of God's existence in creation damages his conscience and hinders his ability to reason.

Rejecting Christ and His redemptive work leads to captivity in a system of lies devised by the devil. When truly accepted and acknowledged, the Word of God benefits us by meeting the deepest needs of our souls. The truth ordained by God for believers enlightens the heart, granting us the assurance of understanding the knowledge of God. We can live free from captivity by acknowledging the mystery of God, the Father, and Christ.

The apostle Paul desired the hearts of the saints to be comforted, knitted together in love, and filled with the riches of full assurance and understanding of the mystery of God (Colossians 2:2-3). Hidden in Christ are all the treasures of wisdom and knowledge for us to live in daily. As clay vessels, we bear this treasure, revealing the overflowing abundance of God's grace, love, and mercy. Recognizing the value of this treasure within us is essential to avoiding captivity.

In 2 Timothy 2:25-26, Paul instructs Timothy to guide those who oppose themselves, praying they may come to repentance and acknowledge the truth. Through this acknowledgment, they can escape the devil's snare and captivity. Ignorance of God's will lead to captivity, so we must not ignore the enemy's devices.

Walking in freedom requires knowledge of the truth. Jesus assured His followers in John 8:32 that knowing the truth would set them free. Being His disciples, we must abide in His truth, allowing His lordship to classify us as followers who partake in the freedom He provides. If the Son sets us free, we are indeed free (John 8:36). Therefore, we must embrace the knowledge of the truth.

As God's people, we experience deliverance through knowing the truth rather than remaining ignorant, which produces bondage. Understanding what God has done for us in Christ brings healing to troubled souls. Proverbs 2:10-11 speaks powerfully, revealing that wisdom and knowledge entering our hearts bring pleasure to our souls, while discretion and understanding preserve and keep us. The entrance of God's Word brings light, granting understanding to the simple (Psalm 119:130). Daily, the light of knowledge shines upon dark mindsets through the preaching of the Gospel, inviting humanity to step out of the captivity of sin and into the glorious liberty of being sons of God through Jesus Christ, our Savior.

Prayer

Lord, I stand in awe of Your divine plan of redemption established from the world's foundation. In Your infinite wisdom, You designed a way for us to be made whole and complete in Christ, who created everything. Your grace has bestowed upon us the unsearchable riches of Christ, revealing the fellowship of the mystery hidden in You from the beginning of time.

I am deeply convinced by the truth that rejecting Christ leads to captivity and the judgment of God. Your Word declares that those who reject You and Your words will face judgment on the last day. Help us, O Lord, to understand the gravity of this rejection, for it distorts our identity and separates us from the intended victory You have provided through Christ.

Gracious God, I acknowledge that Your Word is inspired and profitable for doctrine, reproof, correction, and instruction in righteousness. It is the source of light and truth, revealing Your image in us and pointing us to our completeness in Christ. Yet, so often, humanity dismisses and rejects Your Word, causing significant damage to our ability to reason and understand Your truth.

Father, I implore You to deliver me from the bondage of false teachings and deceptive theories. Your Word alone holds the answers to my deepest needs and desires. I desire to fully embrace and accept the truth it contains, knowing that it is infallible and faithful to my soul's most profound need.

May my heart be comforted, united in love, and filled with the full assurance of understanding. Do not allow me to be ignorant of Your will, that I may avoid the snares and captivities set by the devil.

I yearn to walk in the freedom that comes from knowing the truth. Let Your truth make me genuinely open to the knowledge of Christ and His victory for me. May I never forget the value of the treasure within me, the overflowing abundance of Your grace, love, and mercy.

As I embrace Your wisdom and knowledge, grant me discretion and understanding to navigate life's challenges. Preserve us, O Lord, and keep us from falling, as Your Word becomes a shining light that guides our every step.

Father, through preaching the Gospel, may the light of knowledge penetrate the darkest corners of my mind. May it awaken those held captive in the chains of sin and lead them into the glorious liberty found in Jesus Christ. May we, as Your people, live delivered and free, anchored in the truth and protected by Your Word.

In the mighty name of Jesus, I pray, believing that Your truth will impact our spirits and set us free. In Jesus name, Amen.

Chapter Six:
The Power of Cross Bearing: Embracing Spiritual Transformation

I n the depths of our souls, we hear a divine invitation resonating, beckoning us to embark on a profound journey of spiritual significance. This chapter, titled "Cross Bearing," delves into the depths of our being, igniting a spiritual fire within us and inspiring a transformative connection with the divine. Through powerful verses such as Luke 9:23, Luke 9:62, Matthew 11:28-30, and Matthew 10:38, we unravel the essence of cross-bearing and its profound impact on our spiritual lives.

Embracing the Daily Relationship:

The initial invitation from Jesus encompasses far more than mere words; it encapsulates a call to enter into a daily relationship with Him, marked by self-denial and steadfast commitment. As believers, we find solace and rest in relinquishing worldly pursuits that leave our souls empty and ensnared by deception. Luke 9:25 reminds us of the fleeting nature of material gains, urging us to safeguard our eternal souls instead of chasing transient vanities.

Dying to Self, Embracing the Image:

In taking up our cross daily, we undergo a profound transformation, shedding our former selves and emerging as accurate reflections of Christ's image. Galatians 6:14 testifies to the crucifixion of our worldly desires and the subsequent resurrection of a life entirely devoted to the Father's kingdom. Through this surrender, we rediscover the glory lost in the Garden of Eden, experiencing restoration and connection with God through the redeeming power of Christ's sacrifice.

Knowing His Will, Finding Rest:

We must intimately know His will as we take up our cross and follow Jesus. Matthew 11:28- 30 provides a glimpse into the rewards of being yoked with Christ, finding rest and peace for our weary souls. By learning from Him and taking His yoke upon us, we destroy sin's chains, finding proper stability and rest within the embrace of our Savior.

Putting God First:

When we prioritize the Kingdom of God, a profound shift occurs. Seeking God's kingdom first allows His anointing to flow through us, manifesting His love and glory in our lives. By sharing personal miracles and experiences, we illustrate the abundant rewards of putting God first, enabling us to love others as we are loved.

Identifying with Christ:

In walking the path of cross-bearing, we identify ourselves with Christ, imitating His close relationship with the Father. Just as Jesus proclaimed in John 10:30, "I and my Father are one." We, too, strive to walk in unity with our Heavenly Father, embracing His mission for our lives. By dwelling in Christ and allowing His words to abide in us, we become fruitful branches connected to the divine vine.

Following His Example:

Jesus, the ultimate example of cross-bearing, exemplified unwavering devotion to His Father's will. He constantly proclaimed His identification with the Father and His purpose, never wavering in His mission. In following Jesus, we find our purpose and mission, knowing that as the Father sent Him, He sends us to continue His work on Earth.

Enduring the Cross:

We endure as we take up our cross, just as Jesus did. Hebrews 12:2 reminds us of the joy set before Jesus as he endured the cross, despising the shame, and is now seated at the right hand of the throne of God. We, too, are destined to conquer the challenges, bearing our cross with perseverance and receiving the crown of life promised to us.

The Power of the Gospel:

By embracing cross-bearing, we become vessels of God's glory, transforming lives and overturning darkness. The weight of His glory empowers us to bring forth fruitfulness in barrenness, ushering in a new era of God's righteousness and overcoming sin's grip on humanity. The manifestation of the sons of God unfolds through our obedience and unwavering commitment to the call.

Conclusion:

As we follow the steps of Abraham, the father of faith, we embrace the call to cross-bearing, acknowledging that our beliefs shape our being. Romans 4:12 reveals that we also "walk in the steps of that faith of our father Abraham, which he had yet been uncircumcised." Let us cast aside complacency and apathy, recognizing the urgency of the times and the significance of the cross we bear. Through faith and obedience, we embark on a transformative journey, aligning ourselves with God's will and experiencing the fullness of His promises. The power of cross-bearing resides within us, waiting to be ignited and revealed to the world. In Galatians 6:14, Paul declared: "God forbid that should glory, save in the cross of our Lord Jesus Christ, by whom the world is crucified unto me, and I unto the world."

Prayer

Mighty Father, in the precious name of Jesus, I approach Your throne with reverence and awe. Your Word calls us to take up our cross daily and follow You. This invitation goes beyond a causal relationship; it beckons us to a profound journey of self-denial, fellowship, and submission to Your sovereign rule.

Our souls find rest and satisfaction in walking with You, for You lead us on paths of righteousness and preserve us as Your saints. We rejoice in the separation from the mundane things of life that deceive and rob our souls of our true purpose. We recognize that gaining the whole world at the expense of our souls is a tragic trade-off, while losing ourselves in pursuit of eternal treasures yields immeasurable rewards.

Holy Father, taking up our cross each day means embracing the dying to self, surrendering our will to Yours, and conforming to the image of Christ. As we bear the identification marks of the cross, the world loses its hold on us, and we find true life in fellowship with You. Our lives become crucified to the world, and the world becomes crucified to us as we embrace a life fully surrendered to Your kingdom and purpose.

In Your graciousness, You invite us to come to You, all who labor and are burdened, promising rest for our weary souls. You call us to take Your yoke upon us, to learn from You, for You are gentle and humble in heart. In this yoke of fellowship, we find rest, and Your burden becomes light. Through this intimate connection, You break the yoke of the enemy's captivity and offer us true freedom and stability for our souls.

Putting Your kingdom first in our lives opens the door to experiencing Your love, glory, and miraculous provision. By seeking first Your kingdom and righteousness, we witness the manifestation of Your power, love, and glory in our lives and the lives of those around us. We are empowered to love others as You love us, for Your love enables us to overflow with compassion and generosity.

Holy Father, to follow You means letting go of the past and embracing a new life in Your Word. As we abide engrafted into Your Word, it sanctifies us and transforms us into the image of Christ. We become vessels of Your glory, no longer captive to the world's system but seated in heavenly places with Christ. Your Word guides, empowers, and reveals Your will to us. You have called us to be one with You. Jesus always did the things that pleased You because He lived in perfect obedience to Your will. He identified with You and fulfilled the mission You entrusted to Him. Likewise, You have called us to fulfill that same mission, to be sent into the world as ambassadors of Christ, just as You sent Him. We acknowledge that our lives are not our own but belong to You, and we are here to do Your will.

In the journey of cross-bearing, we see Jesus as the author and finisher of our faith. He endured the cross, despising the shame, and is now seated at Your right hand. We, too, endure hardships, bear our cross, and look to the joy set before us. We press on in faith, knowing that Jesus overcame the world and that our faith in Him leads to the salvation of our souls.

As we follow You into the Kingdom, we witness the power of the Gospel transforming lives, turning wastelands into fertile ground, and manifesting the sons and daughters of God. With the weight of Your glory accompanying us, we become instruments of change, bringing Your righteousness and light into the darkness of this world. We conquer and rest in Your presence, continually empowered to do good and reflect the image of Christ.

Holy Father, like Abraham, the father of faith, we embrace the call to obedience by observing our purpose and timing. We believe in Your promises and step out in faith, even when we cannot see the way. We trust that You are faithful to fulfill what You have spoken, and we walk before You, fully persuaded of Your power and goodness.

May our lives be marked by unwavering faith and obedience as we take up our cross daily and follow You. Let us never be captive to empty pursuits or complacency but remain diligent in fulfilling the Great Commission. Empower us, Lord, to walk in the fullness of our identity in Christ and to be instruments of Your kingdom on earth.

In the name of Jesus, our Savior and Lord. Amen.

Prayer

Almighty and Holy Father, Friend of Abraham, and God of Isaac and Jacob, I humbly approach Your throne in awe and reverence. In the precious name of Jesus, I stand before You, recognizing the marvels of Your power lavished upon me. What a true and faithful friend I have in Jesus, who exemplifies unwavering obedience upon the Mount of the Lord. He endured the weight of the cross, despising its shame, and now sits at Your right hand, adorned with the rewards of His obedience. Through the example of Jesus, I am closer to You, dear Father, witnessing the splendor of His faith and the glory that stems from perfect obedience. By observing His unwavering commitment, I receive the power to partake in His obedience and bask in its transformative glory. Like Abraham, I receive numerous blessings through the covenant of faith.

Father, through Abraham's obedient sacrifice upon the Mount, we witness the manifestation of Your divine provision. In that very hour of obedience, You revealed Yourself as Jehovah-Jireh, providing a ram caught in the thicket as a substitute for his offering. In that moment, a kairos revelation stirred within Abraham's soul, and he confessed You as Jehovah-

Jireh, the God who provides. Oh, the glory and splendor of Your abundant provisions!

Father, just as You captured Abraham's future state as a father of many nations through prophetic words, I understand that You have also caught my destiny in Your promises. With unwavering faith, I stand firm, beholding my future wrapped within Your eternal Word.

Moreover, as I endure the weight of my cross, I am inspired by the life of Moses, who persevered by fixing his eyes on the invisible, knowing that You, the invisible God, were his ultimate reward. You captured my portrait within the sacred Scripture filled with Promises, Purpose, and Prosperity, all interwoven into my very being. The sufferings I endure in bearing my cross at this moment pale compared to the magnificent glory that awaits me. Therefore, with unwavering confidence, I continue to worship and praise You, dear Father, for manifesting Your glory through obedience. I embrace the spiritual impact of cross-bearing and find solace in the footsteps of those who have gone before me. May my life be a testament to Your unwavering love and the transformative power of obedience. In the matchless name of Jesus, I pray. Amen.

Chapter Seven:
The Transformative Power
of Knowledge

In the beginning, God gave Adam knowledge to perceive, recognize, and have an ongoing relationship with him. Proverbs 2:6 states, "For the LORD gives wisdom: out of his mouth cometh knowledge and understanding." The wisdom of God results in knowledge and experience. Adam began speaking by the inspiration God breathed into him. His reverence for his Maker was the beginning of knowledge for him to walk in. Proverbs 1:7 states, "The fear of the LORD is the beginning of knowledge: but fools despise wisdom and instruction."

Genesis 2:7, "And the LORD God formed man of the dust of the ground, and breathed into his nostrils the breath of life; and man became a living soul."

Let us examine the image and likeness God breathed into the first man, Adam, that caused him to reproduce, crowned in the glory immediately after that order.

- God said (Genesis 1:26) Adam said (Genesis 2:23)
- God made (Genesis 1:7) Adam and Eve made (Genesis 3:7)
- God saw (Genesis 1:12) Adam said what he saw (Genesis 2:23)
- God called (Genesis 1:8) Adam called (Genesis 2:19-20)
- God named (Genesis 5:2) Adam named (Genesis 2:20)

In these scriptures, the image and likeness of God manifested in man. Adam and Eve had a perfect union with God and walked developing in His image and likeness daily until sin entered the picture. Romans 5:12 states, "Wherefore, as by one man sin entered into the world, and death by sin; and so death passed upon all men, for that all have sinned." Romans 3:23 states, "For all have sinned, and come short of the glory of God." The first Adam came short of God's glory; the Last Adam, Jesus Christ, restored the glory.

Examining now the image and likeness of God through the last Adam, Jesus Christ, is strikingly profound in expression. As the promised seed in Genesis 3:15, He came forth, walking throughout the New Testament in favor of God and man. The image and likeness of God started in Genesis through the first

Adam. In the New Testament, under the last Adam, Jesus Christ, there is a more profound order of man being a new creature in the image of Christ.

- Jesus, the Christ, cast out devils. (Mark 1:34)
- Man, in Christ, cast out devils. (Acts 16:18)
- Jesus, the Christ, laid hands on the sick, and they recovered. (Luke 4:40)
- Man, in Christ, laid hands on the sick, and they recovered. (Acts 28:8)
- Jesus, the Christ, walked on water. (Matthew 14:26)
- Man, through Christ, walked on water. (Matthew 14:29)
- Jesus, the Christ, had virtue in his body and had virtue in His clothes that healed the sick. (Matthew 9:21)
- Paul, a man, in Christ, from his body were brought unto the sick handkerchiefs or aprons and the diseases departed from them and evil spirits went out of them. (Acts 19:11-12)

The above-listed contrast of believers performing in Christ demonstrates the returned glory in man functioning as fellow laborers with God in His work. We operate through the manifold grace of God. II Corinthians 5:20 states: "Now then we are ambassadors for Christ, as though God did beseech you by us: we pray you in Christ's stead, be ye reconciled to God." Looking further at II Corinthians 6:1, we see: "We then, as workers together with him, beseech you also that ye receive not the grace of God in vain." Again, I want to repeat that life in Christ is a "new becoming" life. Let us awaken to the returned glory that we have in Christ.

Next, I want to recant a story from scripture of the people of God who did not allow the transforming knowledge of God to heal them. In the sacred book of Hosea, we encounter a profound message from God Himself, spoken through the lips of the prophet. These words echo through the ages, piercing the depths of our souls: "My people are destroyed for lack of knowledge." In these few weighty words, we uncover a timeless truth that has shaped the destiny of nations and individuals alike.

Hosea, a faithful servant of God, brings to light the consequence of rejecting knowledge. The children of Israel, whom God had delivered from the bondage of Egypt, were at risk of captivity once again. Their downfall lay not in the unavailability of knowledge but in their willful rejection. By turning their backs on the wisdom and guidance offered by their Creator, they forfeited their role as priests and lost their intimate connection with God.

The path to captivity paved with the stones of ignorance and forgetfulness hinges on captivity. God desired to see the whole house of Judah and Israel rise as a people of praise, glory, and distinction. Yet, they stubbornly refused to listen, allowing their knowledge to wane. The knowledge they rejected determined their destiny, robbing them of their intended purpose and reducing them to captives in the very land where they were to be free.

Israel's lack of knowledge did not stem from its unavailability, for God had graciously provided pastors to feed them His word. The root cause lay in their failure to retain God in their learning. Their minds became entangled in worshipping false gods, and their captivity ensued. Psalm 78 paints a sad picture of Israel's behavior, a tale of hearts gone astray and spirits unsteady in their devotion to God. They disregarded His covenant, refused to walk in His ways, and forgot His marvelous works.

As their rebellion grew, so did their audacity in testing God's patience, demanding fulfillment of their lustful desires. The consequences were dire. The Most High God, provoked by their disobedience and worship of idols, withdrew His favor. The tabernacle of Shiloh, once a symbol of divine presence, was forsaken, and Israel found itself captive, its strength and glory held captive by the enemy's hand. Oh, what a grievous reversal of fortune borne from the rejection of knowledge.

But the descent into captivity did not end there. Israel's captivity deepened as they continued to walk in disobedience, forsaking their glorious status as God's chosen people. They defiled themselves with idolatry, sought counsel from lifeless objects, and their glory turned to shame. Hosea 4:7 reveals the heartbreaking outcome of their rebellion: the Lord changed their glory into shame.

With a voice of righteous concern, the Lord announced His controversy with the land's inhabitants. Truth, mercy, and knowledge of God were scarce commodities. Yet, even during captivity, there was hope. The Lord promised to allure Israel in His boundless mercy, bringing them into the wilderness to speak tenderly to their wounded souls. He offered them vineyards from the barren land, making the Valley of Achor a door of hope. In that place of captivity, He promised them a restoration of their youth and a fresh start, just as they experienced when they came liberated from Egypt's grasp. It is time to be awakened to God's glory today.

The Valley of Achor symbolizes the very place where Israel's captivity began. Yet, it was in that same valley that God promised to make them sing once again. He assured them their failures and captivity would not have the final say. He would lift them from their fallen state, transforming their sorrow into joy and their captivity into freedom. Oh, the depth of His steadfast love and faithfulness!

Let us take heed of the lessons of Israel's journey. Their lack of retaining God in their knowledge led to their downfall, but God, in His mercy, pursued them relentlessly. Even when they lost sight of their redeemed status, He remained faithful, seeking to bring them back to peace and joy in His presence. He saw their thoughts, even from afar, and yearned for them to recognize His mighty works and promises.

But, oh, the danger of negative thoughts and unbelief! Israel's negative proverbs, lack of trust in God's provision, and rejection of His truth brought about their captivity. Their failure to retain God in their knowledge severed their connection to His power and grace. Captivity became their reality.

We, too, must take this to heart. If we neglect the gracious deliverance brought forth by Christ, failing to acknowledge our reconciled state, we risk falling into captivity once more. Just as Israel could not recognize the hand of God working among them, we must not forget His goodness and faithfulness. Let us not be cut short of the glorious destiny that Christ's redemptive work has bestowed upon us.

In the prophetic voice of Hosea, we discover that a lack of knowledge is equivalent to a lack of intimacy—an incomplete spiritual experience. We must cultivate a deep, intimate knowledge of God, engaging in heartfelt dialogue with Him. Our rejection of His knowledge can lead to dire consequences, for it works both ways—when we reject God, He, too, withdraws from us.

Israel's descent into captivity occurred when they attributed their blessings to false gods, forsaking the trustworthy source of their provision. God, in His justice, allowed them to experience the consequences of their disobedience, unveiling the nakedness incurred through their rebellion. Yet, even in judgment, God's purpose was to correct their ways, to bring them back to the truth.

We find solace in knowing that God is a sanctuary amid any captivity. His presence accompanies us even in our darkest moments. He is the faithful Father who relentlessly pursues His children, desiring to deliver us from our waywardness and restore us to His truth. He knows our thoughts, our failures, and our potential. He knows His plans for us, dreams of peace, and an expected end.

Therefore, let us remember that prophecy hangs over our lives, declaring the imminent return of our Lord Jesus Christ. Just as God set forth deliverance for

Israel, He has promised salvation for us. We must hold fast to His word, allowing it to guide our thoughts and actions, for it is in obedience to His will that we find true freedom.

May we never forget the transformative power of knowledge. As we embrace a deep understanding of God's truth and retain Him in our learning, we shall walk in liberty, breaking free from the chains of captivity. Let us cultivate intimacy with God, cherishing His presence and acknowledging His faithfulness. And in the face of any captivity, let us find our refuge in Christ, who holds the key to our liberation.

May our hearts be forever open to the prophetic voice of God, allowing His word to revolutionize our lives and shape our destinies. He calls us to sing amid our captivity, rise from failure into victory, and experience the fullness of His steadfast love. Embrace His truth and let the transformative power of knowledge set you free.

I close this chapter with a personal testimony of how I went about suppressing the knowledge of God in my life. I experienced heartache through a broken marriage and other events in that state of waywardness. Walking without considering God's wisdom for my life was very painful. I was drifting down a dark path of immorality. I remember I went out to a club one night, and I felt so uncomfortable. A gentleman approached me and said, "You don't belong in a place like this." The Lord was using him to speak to me. He could tell I did not fit in with the crowd. I accepted his words and never went back. It took a few more years of living in darkness before the light of Christ shined in me. The Lord pursued me until I felt guilty about my ways of living. I thank God that He delivered me from a sinful lifestyle. Today, I stand through His grace and mercy awaken to my identity in Christ.

Prayer

Gracious and Almighty God, we stand before You, amazed by the timeless truth revealed in the sacred book of Hosea. Your words echo through the ages, piercing the depths of our souls: "My people are destroyed for lack of knowledge." Today, we humbly acknowledge the weight and significance of this truth.

As we reflect on the journey of Israel, we recognize the consequences of rejecting knowledge. In their rebellion, they forfeited their role as priests and lost their intimate connection with You. Ignorance and forgetfulness became their stumbling stones, forcing them not to possess the power they could have kept.

Lord, may we learn from their example and hold tightly to the wisdom and guidance You have graciously provided. Help us retain Your presence in our hearts and minds, refusing to be swayed by this world's false gods and distractions. Let us never forget Your marvelous works and the covenant You have established with us.

During captivity, You, O Lord, are our refuge. Just as You promised restoration to Israel, we cling to the hope that You will transform our sorrows into joy. Grant us the strength to overcome negative thoughts and unbelief so that we may fully embrace the deliverance brought forth by Christ.

Father, we acknowledge the intimacy and spiritual experience of knowing You. May we cultivate a deep and heartfelt knowledge of Your truth, engaging in dialogue with You and cherishing Your presence. Let us not be cut short from the destiny You have ordained for us.

In the face of any captivity, may Your word be our guide and Your faithfulness our anchor. We surrender ourselves to Your divine purpose, recognizing that prophecy hangs over our lives, declaring the imminent return of our Savior, Jesus Christ. Grant us the wisdom and strength to walk obediently and experience true freedom.

Today, we embrace the transformative power of knowledge. Help us retain Your truth, shaping our thoughts, actions, and destiny. May we find refuge in Christ every season, singing songs of victory and rising from failure into the fullness of Your love.

We offer this prayer with hearts wide open to Your prophetic voice. Revolutionize our lives, O God, as we remain focused through the power of Your knowledge. In Jesus' mighty name. Amen.

Part 3: Breaking Free and Moving Forward

Chapter Eight:
Shutting the Door to the
Past

The Power of Letting Go

In this thought-provoking chapter titled "Shutting the Door to the Past," I am using the powerful words of Apostle Paul in Philippians 3:13-14 to serve as the foundation. Paul emphasizes the importance of leaving behind past achievements and embracing God's high calling in Christ Jesus. I highlight the need for closure in various life events and encourage you to trust that everything works together for good. I emphasize the significance of clearing out the old and welcoming new beginnings, finding freedom in Christ and the abundance of life He offers. In this chapter, I emphasize shutting the door to past hurts, denying them access to the mind, and resolving painful moments with closure. I emphasize also that believers are no longer captive to their pasts but are alive in Christ, with a new identity and victory over sin. I conclude with a personal testimony of my experience shutting the door to my past, filled with failures, by demonstrating the transformative power of embracing a new future.

Renewing the Mind:

Inspired by Philippians 3:13-14, letting go of the past and embracing a new life in Christ changes our perspective. Apostle Paul is an example, as he consciously decided to leave behind his previous accomplishments and pursue his calling in Christ. As believers, we need to find closure in moments of tragedy or life-altering events, understanding that God can work all things together for our good. By shutting the door to the past, renewing the mind, and embracing our new identity in Christ, be encouraged to break free from the captivity of the past and step into the abundant life and freedom found in walking with Christ. Paul encourages believers to forget the past and focus on the knowledge of Christ Jesus, emphasizing the importance of renewing our minds. When facing difficult situations, we can refresh our minds and trust that everything will work together for good.

Closure and Moving Forward:

It is time to let go of the old and embrace the new, becoming trophies of God's grace and experiencing seasons of growth where old things die out and fresh life blossoms.

By closing the doors to our past, we create space for God to open doors to a more rewarding life on earth.

The Portal of Heaven's Riches:

Through Christ, we have daily access to God and can explore the vastness of His unsearchable riches, finding treasures and blessings along the way.

By walking through the open door of life in Christ, we enter the abundance and richness of God's kingdom.

Breaking the Chains of Captivity:

To overcome past hurts, we must consciously shut the door on them, denying them access to our minds and allowing Christ's victory to set us free.

Jesus bore our griefs and sorrows, giving us liberation from spiritual death and the power to break free from captivity.

Releasing the Old, Embracing the New:

Our identity in Christ gives us a fresh perspective, enabling us to discover new levels of victory and success.

The broken cistern of our past no longer has power over us, as we are now forgiven in Christ, embracing the newness of life that He offers.

Embracing Your New Life:

Being awakened in Christ is no longer detained by sin, and we experience a release from the law of sin and death.

We can confidently declare our redemption and walk into a new chapter of freedom in Christ, making His freedom the foundation for our daily lives.

The Power of Letting Go, My Testimony:

I want to conclude this chapter by sharing a personal revelation of how the Lord guided me to close the door to a past filled with shame and pain. One day, as I returned home from work and walked down the hallway to my bedroom, I heard the sound of a door shutting in my bosom as I passed the first bedroom. It was a divine moment as the Spirit of the Lord spoke, saying, "Shut the door to your past." Walking further down the hallway, I noticed the second bedroom door was open, and the Spirit instructed me to close it as well. He revealed that although everything in the room was still there when I shut the door, it was out of sight. This experience was pivotal for me to understand that the door to my past was closed by God, and only by choice, if I chose to open it again, did it exist.

On another occasion, I also dreamed of my ex-husband, adorned in a beautiful burgundy suit, speaking to influence me from his coffin. Even after our divorce, his influence lingered, constantly reminding me of our past and what went wrong. But the Lord made it clear that I shouldn't be affected by the voice of someone who was no longer part of my life. That dream further solidified my freedom from a past that no longer served me. The choice was mine to find strength and move forward into the future that awaited me. Praise God, I made that choice.

Prayer

Heavenly Father, in the depths of our hearts, we yearn to shut the door to our past and embrace the new life You have prepared for us. Just as Apostle Paul declared in Philippians 3:13, we forget the things behind us and press forward toward the high calling in Christ Jesus.

Lord, help us to release the grip of our past accomplishments, failures, and hurts. Grant us the courage to leave behind what no longer serves Your purpose for our lives. We surrender our past failures, disappointments, and regrets into Your hands, knowing that You have borne our griefs and sorrows.

As we close the door to our past, we ask for Your grace and strength to renew our minds. Help us discern what we allow into the storage bin of our thoughts, safeguarding that only words, memories, and images that align with Your truth find a place within us. May our minds be transformed by the power of Your Word and the reality of our new identity in Christ.

We thank You, Lord, for our freedom in Christ Jesus. By Your grace, we are no longer captive to our past lives of sin and defeat. We embrace our redemption and reconciliation with You. Empower us to walk confidently in our new identity, declaring Your victory over every aspect of our past.

Every moment reminds us of our breathtaking breathing room in Christ. Please help us to recognize the vastness of potential functionality and freedom that flows in us. Let our lives be a testament to the liberty found in Christ as we boldly declare our redemption and share our stories of transformation.

Today, we choose to re-enter life through Christ, leaving behind the broken cisterns of our past. We declare that the old has passed away, and we are made new in Christ. We hold fast to the truth that we are no longer defined by who we were but by who we are now in Christ.

As we shut the door to our past, we thank You for the illustration and dream You gave to guide us on this journey. We embrace the sound of the closing door and the revelation that everything in the room of our past remains there, unseen and unimportant. We gain strength and move forward into the future You have prepared for us.

Thank You, Lord, for Your faithfulness and the freedom we find in You. We walk in the assurance of Your love, grace, and forgiveness. May our lives testify to the transformation that comes when we shut the door to our past and embrace the fullness of life in Christ.

In Jesus' name, Amen.

Chapter Nine:
Coming out of Dry Places

saiah 44:3: "For I will pour water upon him that is thirsty, and floods upon the dry ground: I will pour my spirit upon thy seed, and my blessing upon thine offspring."

Job 22:29: "When men are cast down, then thou shalt say, There is lifting..."

Renewing the Mind:

During life's changes and disappointments, we may find ourselves in dry places, feeling depleted and thirsty for change. But we can overcome these challenges by renewing our minds and trusting that God will work everything together for our good.

Closure and Moving Forward:

To come out of the dry places of weariness, loneliness, and emptiness, we need to seek closure to the past and embrace the new opportunities and blessings God has in store. It's time to let go of the weight of our past and step into the future with faith and determination.

The Portal of Heaven's Riches:

In pursuing a fulfilling life, we must recognize that God's kingdom is open to us, overflowing with blessings and opportunities. By closing the doors to our past and walking through the door of life in Christ, we can access the vastness of God's unsearchable riches.

Breaking the Chains of Captivity:

Dry places can represent captivity, where we feel trapped by past hurts, failures, or wrong mindsets. However, through Christ, we can break free from these chains of captivity and experience true liberation. Through the knowledge of Christ and the guidance of the Holy Spirit, we find our way to freedom.

Releasing the Old, Embracing the New:

Our past no longer defines us; we have a new identity and life in Christ. Letting go of the old and embracing the new enables us to walk in the fullness of God's grace and experience the freedom and abundance He has prepared for us.

Personal Testimony: Embracing My New Life

Through personal testimony, I share how I emerged from a dry place. From a life wasted in sin to the redemption and ministry found in Christ, I discovered the power of surrendering to His purpose. During dry seasons, you can find strength and restoration through the Word of God, faith, and obedience.

Coming out of dry places is about overcoming past hurts or failures, embracing the present moment, and living in the fullness of what God has for you. By renewing your mind, seeking closure, and trusting in God's promises, you can experience a transformation that leads to a life of joy, purpose, and abundance. Decide to leave the dry places, leave the past behind, and walk confidently into the future God has prepared for you.

Testimony - From Dryness to Deliverance

In the depths of weariness, loneliness, emptiness, and self-destruction, there comes a divinely appointed time when God pours out His love upon us. He knows how to lead us out of the dry places and into the warmth of His embrace. In this chapter, I want to share a heartfelt testimony of how I found deliverance from the dryness that once consumed my life.

A Life Wasted in Sin:

Born into a Christian home as the seventh child among nine siblings, I drifted away from God's Word. Unaware of the deep darkness that awaited me, I spiraled into a life of sin, experiencing countless dry places. Little did I know that the prayers of my parents and the grace of God were working behind the scenes, calling me back to the path of redemption.

Divine Intervention and Protection:

In my despair, a pivotal moment would forever change my life. As I sat in our living room, consumed by alcohol and devising a plan to confront my husband, a divine intervention occurred. My parents' faces appeared before me on the front of our plastic-covered sofa, their mouths silently saying, "No." It was a powerful message from the Lord, preventing me from entering danger. Only later did I learn that my husband had intended to harm me. God's grace and the prayers of my parents had shielded me from impending disaster so that I could not go through with what I had planned.

A Season of Restoration:

After eight and a half years of marriage, our relationship ended in divorce. I found myself on the welfare system, raising our four children alone. Yet, amidst the challenges, God was at work, using those welfare years to prepare for a new chapter in our lives. Through the faithful touch of Christ, my thought life and prayer life transformed. He birthed a ministry of teaching His Word within me and filled me with the Holy Spirit, igniting a daily longing to honor and glorify His name.

A Turning Point:

In November 1972, I experienced a profound change from a place of dryness to discovering God's purpose for my life. I surrendered my heart to Jesus Christ, realizing He had been waiting to enrich and adorn me with His glory and virtue. It was time for me to reclaim the identity that God had planned for me in Christ. My journey began with immersing myself in the Word of God, reprogramming my mind with the promises of His love and grace. The Scriptures became my sustenance, and I discovered the power of Jesus' words as life-giving and spirit-filled.

Overcoming Adversity:

As I obeyed God's Word, strength flowed into the dry places of my loneliness and the wounds inflicted by divorce and other painful events. I started experiencing a remarkable lifting and restoration in my life. However, the journey was not without further trials. During a visit with my children to visit their father and grandmother, circumstances unfolded that threatened to separate them. In desperation, I sought guidance from the Lord at a church altar. While waiting for the minister to get to me standing in line, I asked the Lord what I was to ask for. The Lord told me, "Tell him you need to make a decision." In a decisive moment of divine confirmation, before I could tell the minister what I was standing there for, the Minister echoed the Spirit's words to me; he said I hear the Spirit of the Lord saying: "DECISION, DECISION." It was such a moment in the Spirit that I could not stand on my feet. When I could stand back up, the Lord had given me the peace to leave my children with their father and trust His plan for their future. Even though their father told me I could take our two sons because he would keep our two daughters, the Lord gave me peace at that altar to leave all of them with their father.

Trusting God in the Wilderness:

Returning home without my children was agonizing, but the Holy Spirit led me to enroll in college and prepare for my future. Through faith and unwavering trust, I held onto the promise that God would reunite us. And one morning, as I had waited for that long-awaited day, my children arrived at the train station in Wilson, NC. However, the college had scheduled me to pick up my schedule the same morning. When I arrived on campus, the line was so long that I knew I could not wait in that long line. God's faithfulness showed up, and He orchestrated circumstances beyond my control, even granting someone to pass me a pass to bypass the long line at the college and be there in Wilson for my children on time. In that moment, I witnessed the beginning of a transformation within myself and my children's lives. God's faithfulness prevailed!

Prosperity in Adversity:

As my children embarked on their college journeys, I saw the pain of my divorce fading away. Their accomplishments became a flourishing testament to the abundant life God had prepared for them. I realized that God's prosperity extended far beyond material wealth. He was prospering me in the prosperity of the saints, healing the wounds of the past, and restoring hope for a brighter future.

A Call to Live:

Amidst the dry places, I learned the profound truth of Psalm 3:3 that the Lord is my shield, my glory, and the lifter of my head. With this resolve, I prophesied to myself, declaring that I would no longer stay "stuck on stuck." I embraced the lifting and shifting that God had prepared for me. Even in the face of adversity, I refused to remain captive to my past. Instead, I chose to be strong, to live fully, and to honor God with my life.

Leaving Dryness Behind:

Through my journey, I have emerged from countless dry places. I have learned to decree and declare that God works all things together for our good, even transforming what seemed evil into blessings beyond measure. I urge you to do the same. Refuse to be defined by your past and open yourself to the beauty that awaits you in the Lord. Embrace the restoration, the healing, and the new beginning God has prepared for you.

Dry places should not feel permanent but temporary because they are seasons that lead us to a deeper understanding of God's love and purpose for our lives. As we trust in His guidance, seek renewal of our minds, and step into His abundant grace, we can emerge from the dry places with a renewed spirit and a testimony of His faithfulness. May this testimony inspire you to believe that no matter how dry your circumstances may be, God can bring forth rivers of living water and lead you into a life overflowing with His love, joy, and fulfillment.

Do not despise your dry season, for it holds a blessing that can propel you into a new growth phase. Your dry place can transform into a place of healing if you understand that God allows it to open you up to a season of renewed zeal and strength. It is time for you to step into your next season and let go of the pain of the past. Release the weight of previous failures and disappointments. Close the door to your past, opening the door to your new beginning. Your past may try to linger in your present, but you must rise above it and think on a higher level to start afresh.

To recover from a dry place, follow three essential steps: examine the root cause of the dryness and repent, seek freedom through the Word of God and in Christ, and trust in God's grace to rescue you from the enemy's snare. By understanding and applying the knowledge of Christ, you can overcome wrong mindsets and find recovery through repentance. God's thoughts toward you are always purposeful and sound, just as He showed the captives in Babylon. He said unto those captives in Jeremiah 29:11: "For I know the thoughts that I think towards you, saith the LORD, thoughts of peace, and not evil, to give you an expected end." Even in dry places, God's plans for you are for peace and a hopeful future.

You are more than a conqueror through Christ, and by putting on the armor of God, you can avoid falling into captivity. Embrace your identity in Christ, saying no to anything that contradicts the knowledge of God. Upgrade your thought life, shifting from thoughts that hold you back to thoughts that uplift and set you up for an abundant life. You have a call to live in the present moment, so let go of the past and experience victory today.

In conclusion, seize the present moment and refuse to lose any more time dwelling on the past. Embrace the freedom and liberty Christ has given you and say yes to life in Him. Pray the prayer below of commitment as you close this chapter, affirming your determination to leave the dry place behind and embrace the abundant life God has prepared for you.

Prayer

Heavenly Father, I come before You with a heart filled with gratitude and hope. Thank You for the wisdom and encouragement I have received through Your Word. Today, I know You have a purpose for every season of my life, even the dry and challenging ones.

Lord, I confess that there have been moments when I despised my dry season, allowing it to weigh me down and steal my joy. But I now realize that You have allowed this season to open me up to a new phase of growth and transformation. Help me to see the blessings hidden within the dryness and grant me the strength to embrace the lessons and opportunities it presents.

I release the pain of the past and the burden of my failures. By the power of Your Holy Spirit, cleanse my mind from dwelling on negative thoughts and replaying old tapes of hurt and disappointment. Lead me into the joy of forgiveness and the freedom from surrendering all to You.

I surrender the root causes of dryness in my life to You, dear Lord. Show me any areas where I need to repent and make amends. Guide me to escape any chains that hold me captive, using Your Word as my guide and source of strength. Help me trust in Your grace to rescue me from the enemy's snares.

I thank You for the knowledge of Christ that empowers me to cast down every imagination and thought that opposes Your truth. Please grant me the discernment to recognize false perspectives and the humility to correct my thinking through repentance. May I recover and walk in the victory You have already secured through Christ.

Father, I hold on to the promise that You know your thoughts toward me. Just as You brought healing and peace to the captives in Babylon, I trust that You have good plans for my life. Grant me the wisdom to settle and flourish in my current circumstances, knowing that You are working all things together for my good.

I declare that I am more than a conqueror through Christ. I have put on Your armor so that I may stand firm against the enemy's schemes. Please help me to live in the present moment, fully alive and free from the bondage of the past. Let this day be a new beginning, filled with intense happiness and purpose.

I surrender my past, present, and future into Your loving hands. Guide me each step of the way as I embrace the abundant life You have prepared for me. I choose to say yes to life in Christ, to live in liberty, and to walk in the fullness of Your grace. In Jesus' name, I pray. Amen.

Chapter Ten:
Caught in the Thicket of
a Wilderness of Flesh

The Dual Walk: Spirit vs. Flesh

Within Romans chapter 8, we are confronted with the choice to walk in the Spirit or the flesh. The solution to this struggle, Galatians 3:16, reveals that we are encouraged to walk in the Spirit, ensuring that the lust of the flesh does not become dominant over us. Ephesians 5:15 reminds us to walk circumspectly, redeeming the time amidst the evil days.

Entangled in the Thicket:

The term "thicket" symbolizes the entanglement, entwinement, and bondage we may find ourselves trapped in—a complex maze of destructive patterns. Simultaneously, the wilderness represents a bewildering state where fleshly desires drive our talk and actions. If we walk not in the Spirit, Galatians 5:17 emphasizes the conflict between the flesh and the Spirit, interweaving with our words and steps and leading us deeper into the thicket of a wilderness of flesh.

The Power of Speech: A Soul-Trapping Wilderness

When our speech becomes entangled in a wilderness that traps the soul, it reflects a mindset focused on carnal thoughts rather than spiritual understanding. Romans 8:6 draws attention to the consequence of a carnal mind—death, while a spiritual mind leads to life and peace. James 3:10 warns against the contradiction of a fountain that produces sensual and spiritual talk, blessing, and cursing. Our words have the potential to foster bitterness, envy, and strife in our hearts.

The Tongue: A Tool of Liberation or Entrapment

The Book of Proverbs contains profound wisdom regarding the tongue and its remarkable power to trap or liberate. Proverbs emphasize the potential snaring by the words of our mouths (6:2) and the joy that comes from speaking wisely (15:23). It distinguishes between righteous lips, indicating wisdom (16:13), and lying lips, pointing to wickedness (12:22). The impact of speech supports improving the heart with excellent words (15:13) or entangling it with a perverse tongue (15:4). Proverbs 18:21 sums up the profound truth that death and life reside within the power of the tongue. Those who love it will experience the fruit thereof.

Choosing the Right Words: The Path to Freedom

Through the lens of Proverbs, we comprehend that we can speak in a way that aligns with either righteousness or unrighteousness as we dwell in these earthly bodies. Job 6:25 reminds us of the forcefulness of correct words, while Jesus warns in Matthew 12:37 that we will be justified or condemned based on our words. Let us choose not to perish in the wilderness, trapped by wrong words, reminiscent of the Children of Israel whose mouths caused their downfall.

The Heart's Influence: From Abundance to Utterance

Jesus confirms the link between the heart and the words we speak, questioning how we, being evil, can utter good things. He emphasizes that our words emanate from the abundance of our hearts. James 3:6 explicitly declares that the tongue has the power to defile the entire body and direct the course of our lives. James 3:8 describes the tongue as an unruly evil, full of deadly poison. These profound spiritual truths unveil the danger of speaking ourselves into the thicket of a wilderness of flesh. Repentance becomes the pathway to purify our hearts and restore a renewed vocabulary.

Transforming Thoughts: The Foundation of Speech

The foundation of our spoken words lies within our thought lives. Wrong thinking leads to irresponsible speech. We should carefully think before we speak, preventing the destruction of nature against us, as Moses demonstrated in the wilderness. His provoked spirit resulted in an unadvised speech to the children of Israel, leading to dire consequences (Psalm 106:33). James 1:19 encourages us to be swift to hear, slow to speak, and slow to wrath, as the wrath of man does not produce the righteousness of God.

Embracing the Call to Truth:

Life is a journey of living and breathing in the truth. The Father seeks genuine worshippers who have accepted the call to walk in truth. We must examine our speech and actions, acknowledging that we may still make carnal decisions. However, we are encouraged to transcend the desires of the flesh, the lust of the eyes, the lust of the flesh, and the pride of life. By embracing the knowledge of Christ, we escape the world's pollution and find freedom through our Lord and Savior, Jesus Christ, as II Peter 2:18-22 affirms.

In each chapter of *AWAKENED IDENTITY NO LONGER A CAPTIVE*, I strive to inspire you to explore and examine your lives, thoughts, speech, and actions. It calls for repentance, renewed thinking, and a deeper walk in the Spirit. By embracing the truths presented, you can break free from the thicket of the wilderness of flesh and live a life aligned with God's will and purpose. Be awakened to your new identity in Christ.

Prayer

Heavenly Father, we come before Your divine presence in this moment of reverence and surrender. We acknowledge that all in the world—the lust of the flesh, the lust of the eyes, and the pride of life—is not of You but of the world. We yearn to be free from the entanglements of the flesh and the bewildering wilderness of the world's systems surrounding us.

Gracious God, we recognize the battle between the Spirit and the flesh within us. We confess that, at times, we have succumbed to the desires of the flesh, losing sight of Your truth and ways. But we now declare our commitment to walk in the Spirit, guided by Your holy presence. Grant us the wisdom to walk circumspectly, as wise and not as fools, redeeming the time in these challenging and evil days.

Lord, we acknowledge the power of our speech—the words that can either trap our souls or liberate us. Help us guard our tongues and fill our hearts with Your wisdom. May our words reflect the spiritual-mindedness that leads to life and peace rather than the carnal-mindedness that tends towards death. May our speech be a source of blessings, free from bitter envy and strife, as we allow Your truth to shape our words.

In the depths of Your wisdom in the Book of Proverbs, we find the keys to taming our tongues and utilizing the power of our tongues for good. We recognize that death and life reside within the power of the tongue, and we desire to choose life, blessing, and enlightenment with every word we speak. Grant us discernment and self-control to use our words to bring healing, encouragement, and truth to those around us.

Dear Lord, we acknowledge that our thoughts are the foundation of our speech. We confess that our thinking has not always aligned with Your truth, leading us to speak unadvisedly and bring harm to ourselves and others. We humbly ask for Your forgiveness and guidance to transform our thought patterns. Help us to be swift to hear, slow to speak, and slow to anger, for we desire to exhibit the righteousness that flows from Your Spirit.

Father, we surrender our lives and tongues to Your loving and refining touch. Purify our hearts, renew our minds, and fill us with Your Holy Spirit. May the words we speak reflect Your truth, love, and grace. Empower us to resist the temptations of the flesh, the lust of the eyes, the lust of the flesh, and the pride of life. Lead us into a more profound knowledge of Your

Son, Jesus Christ, so that we may escape the world's pollution and live a life pleasing to You.

We offer this prayer with our hearts open and surrender to Your will. May it be a catalyst for transformation as we seek to walk in the Spirit and overcome the thicket of the wilderness of flesh. In the mighty and precious name of Jesus. Amen.

Chapter Eleven: Reversing the Course of Your Life

Scripture References: II Corinthians 5:17, Isaiah 54:17, Proverbs 15:23, James 3:6, James 3:2, Proverbs 19:21, Romans 8:28

In the depths of our souls, we yearn for a transformation, a reversal of our lives, to become more fruitful. The desire to see life through a different lens, to make changes, and to embrace a new perspective resonates within us. At the very core, reversing the course of our lives requires a shift in behavior and a fresh desire to view our existence through the lens of Christ, the Redeemer of all humanity.

Examining the Elements of Captivity

To reverse the course of our lives, we must first examine the choices that led us to our current situation. If disorder and unrest prevail, let us look at our daily thoughts. Do our thought patterns align with the Word of God, which proclaims that we are new creatures in Christ? Is it not time to experience the newness promised to us as believers?

The Power of Words

Proverbs 15:23 reminds us of the joy that springs forth from the answers of our mouths and the profound impact of timely spoken words. When we use our mouths to respond to our circumstances with the right words, we set our lives on a new course. Speaking words of life and truth navigates the very fabric of nature, shaping our outcomes. Reversing the course of our lives necessitates a revision, an adjustment, and a correction in our words, freeing us from the captivity of stagnation.

The Transformative Power of Right Thinking

James 3:6 warns us about the destructive potential of the tongue, highlighting the need for self-control and the ability to bridle our words. Furthermore, James 3:2 emphasizes the significance of guarding our tongues to become complete individuals, enabling us to discipline our entire beings. Our minds, too, require a recovery journey involving the renewal of thought patterns. By adopting right-thinking patterns, we mold and shape our minds to align with God's truth and holiness. Our thoughts can shape our lives, either confining us to a lower existence or propelling us toward a higher purpose. Let us choose healing and victorious words of life to renew our hearts' thoughts.

Embracing Our Heritage

Always remember that as servants of the Lord, we possess a heritage that grants us the authority to counter and overturn the negative words spoken against us. Isaiah 54:17 assures us that no weapon formed against us shall prosper, and every tongue raised in judgment shall be proven wrong. Our heritage as children of God is peace, righteousness, security, and a decisive triumph over opposition. This promise is woven into the fabric of our everyday lives and has been proven true by countless believers.

Personal Testimony: From Struggles to Abundance: Embracing God's Promises

In the depths of my struggles and heartbreak, I discovered a lifeline in the power of Isaiah 54:17. I refused to accept the lie that, as a divorcee with four children, I would be a destined failure. Instead, I chose to walk by faith and embrace the promise that no weapon formed against me would prosper. This decision transformed my life and led me on a remarkable journey of triumph and flourishing in God's abundant blessings.

I defied the odds with unwavering faith and overcame the lie that threatened to overshadow my path. I stepped into the fullness of God's favor, experiencing the manifestation of His promises in my life. My journey was marked by prosperity, fulfilling long-held dreams, and establishing a fruitful ministry.

The Lord's favor became my guiding light, transforming my sorrow into rivers of peace, joy, and hope. Despite my challenges, I witnessed the hand of God moving mightily, blessing me and my family in extraordinary ways. All four of my children not only graduated from four-year colleges but excelled in their educational pursuits. In a testament to God's faithfulness, I graduated from Bible College, attaining a Doctoral Degree in Theology.

But the story doesn't end there. God's favor continued to follow me, leading me into new realms of influence and impact. I became the Founder and President of a Bible College, empowering and equipping future generations of leaders in the faith. Additionally, I answered the call to serve as the Founder and Pastor of a local church, ministering to the spiritual needs of my community.

Through it all, I have experienced the abundant rivers of peace, joy, and hope that flow from God's presence. His favor has been my constant companion, opening doors and orchestrating divine connections. My life is a testimony to the transformative power of God's promises when embraced with unwavering faith.

Learning from Esther and Mordecai

In the Old Testament, Esther and Mordecai's story reveals their courageous reversal of a weapon formed against them. Despite a decree to destroy all Jews in the land, they took action and petitioned the king for favor. They had the privilege of rewriting their destiny by changing what another had influenced. Today, we must recognize the importance of wisdom and the power to change what is contrary to our identity in Christ. Like Esther and Mordecai, let us boldly move forward, rewriting the script of our lives.

A Personal Testimony: Divine Protection, Overcoming Adversities through God's Counsel

Proverbs 19:21 holds a profound truth that has profoundly impacted my life. In a situation designed to work against me, the Lord led me to embrace this powerful verse. It was a moment of divine intervention when my deceased ex-husband orchestrated a trap, intending to confront me with his girlfriend at his mother's house. But little did he know that God's counsel would prevail, and His protection would shield me from harm.

During this challenging circumstance, the presence of the Holy Spirit within me became instantly recognizable. After leaving the scene, I felt a surge of praise and hallelujahs welling in my spirit. The surge of hallelujahs in my spirit indicated that the plan to trap and harm me had become powerless and ineffective. The Holy Spirit assured me that the attack against my life had been futile. At that time, He also had me turn to Proverbs 19:21 to let me see there are many devices in a man's heart, but the counsel of the Lord shall stand.

This experience was a powerful reminder of the Lord's favor and protection, working tirelessly in my life. Repeatedly, I have witnessed His hand at work, guarding me from the schemes and attacks of the enemy. He has proven Himself faithful, ensuring that His counsel prevails despite the plans that arise in the hearts of individuals.

Through this encounter, I understand the significance of standing firm in faith when faced with adversities. The Lord's counsel is unshakable, and His protection is unwavering. No matter what schemes or attacks may come against us, we can find refuge in His presence and trust in His divine intervention.

Let us draw strength from Proverbs 19:21, knowing that His plans for us will always supersede any procedures set up to work against us. Through unwavering faith and reliance on His wisdom, we can navigate through adversities, secure in the knowledge that His protection and favor are continually at work. Continue to be inspired and empowered as we delve deeper into how God's counsel prevails and learn to stand firm in His unshakable truth.

The Promise of All Things Working Together

Romans 8:28 reassures us that even in the face of adversity, God can work all things together for our good. As we seek to reverse the course of our lives, let this promise resonate within us, serving as daily nourishment. The impact of God's love speaking to the deepest needs of our hearts becomes the catalyst for rewriting the chapters of our lives.

The call to reverse the course of our lives beckons us to embrace divine transformation. As we examine the elements of captivity, harness the power of our words, transform our thinking patterns, and stand on the promises of our heritage, we find the strength to change the script of our lives. Let the counsel of the Lord guide us, knowing that all things, even adversities, work together for our good. Embrace the transformative power of Christ, rewriting your story with the assurance that old things have passed away, and behold, all things have become new.

Prayer

Heavenly Father, in the depths of our souls, we long for a reversal of the course of our lives. We yearn to see life through the lens of Christ, embracing divine transformation. Today, we come before You, recognizing that old things have passed away and all things have become new in Christ.

Lord, we acknowledge that captivity is not Your desire for us. Please help us to examine the choices we have made and the thoughts we entertain daily. May our thought lives align with Your Word, affirming our identity as new creatures in Christ. Grant us the strength to make changes and speak life-giving words that navigate our lives toward Your divine purpose.

We ask for a renewal of our minds to embrace right-thinking patterns. Mold and shape our thoughts to be aligned with Your truth and holiness. Empower us to reject negative thoughts and embrace victorious thoughts that lead to healing and a higher existence in You.

We hold fast to the promise of our heritage, knowing that no weapon formed against us shall prosper. Every tongue raised against us in judgment, we condemn in the name of Jesus. Your peace, righteousness, security, and triumph over opposition are our inheritance; we receive them with grateful hearts.

Like Esther and Mordecai, we boldly step forward, rewriting the script of our lives. Grant us wisdom and discernment to counter anything contrary to Your plan for us. May we experience the transformative power of Your counsel and the assurance that all things work together for our good.

May Your love speak tenderly and powerfully to the depths of our hearts in every moment of our lives. Help us to embrace divine transformation, rewriting the chapters of our lives according to Your will. We surrender ourselves to You, trusting in Your faithfulness and guidance.

Thank You, Heavenly Father, for listening to our prayer by giving power and impact to them. We know You are working things together for good, reversing the course of our lives and leading us into the fullness of Your purpose. In Jesus' name. Amen.

Part 4: Deepening Spiritual Connection

Chapter Twelve: Heard of God

Prayer: A Source of Confidence and Fellowship

Within the realm of prayer, we find an essential component of our worship—a deepening confidence in God's ability to answer our heartfelt petitions. As we engage in worship through prayer, we enter a sacred fellowship with the Almighty, bringing our requests under the encompassing power of His mercy. We recognize that through Christ, we are seen as righteous before God, seated with Him before the throne of grace. Prayer becomes personal in this place of humility and grace, and God graciously rewards us openly.

Praying According to God's Will and the Efficacy of Christ's Redemption

When we approach God the Father in the name of Jesus, we remind Him of His promises and His willingness to receive us in times of need. Through the redemptive work of Christ's blood, our prayers find a guaranteed audience in heaven. They are likened to golden vials, emitting a fragrant aroma before the throne of God. Through the intercession of Jesus, we present our highest glory and salvation in prayer. Be assured that God hears and answers our heartfelt cries. Therefore, let us persevere in prayer, knowing He delights in our persistent communication with Him.

Experiences of Personal Answered Prayer

I have encountered the profound reality of God's responsiveness to my prayers. Once, while desiring reconciliation with my husband, I placed my faith in God's hands, uttering a prayer of trust and surrender. I asked the Lord to keep my husband away if his intentions conflicted with our well-being. In His wisdom, God arranged for my husband's visit not to happen. At that moment, the Spirit directed me to 1 John 5:14, and I realized that our prayer receives answers when aligned with God's will. This experience etched in my heart the undeniable reality of God's involvement in answering my prayers.

On another occasion, as I knelt before God in prayer, His presence manifested and shrouded like a cloud upon me in my bedroom. He invited me to ask for anything I desired. Overwhelmed, I pondered what to ask, and the presence began to lift from before me. Realizing His presence was rising from before me, I immediately asked for wisdom and knowledge to lead His people in and out. My words appeared captured and went up in the clouds to heaven. Later, I discovered that Solomon had a similar encounter in I Kings 3:5. That event has prepared me with God's wisdom and knowledge in my pastoral role. It is a gift the Lord gave me.

Prayer: A Territory of Wisdom and Knowledge

Prayer is not merely a formality; it is a territory we must occupy with the wisdom and knowledge of God. We present His Word before Him, acknowledging its truth within our hearts. He has appointed an accepted time for us to bring our requests before Him, and to neglect this power is to underestimate the authority He has bestowed upon our prayers. We are reminded in James 4:2 that we often lack because we fail to ask.

Asking the Father in Jesus' Name and the Holy Spirit's Help in Prayer

Jesus Himself emphasized the power of asking the Father in His name. He has assured us that our Father will hear whatever we ask in His name. In our times of prayer before our Heavenly Father, the Holy Spirit also assists us in praying for things we struggle to articulate. We can rely on the Holy Spirit's guidance and intercession as we communicate with God.

The Petition Welcomed and Heard by the Father

When we approach the throne of grace, let us understand that our Heavenly Father receives the petitions we bring before Him. In 2 Corinthians 6:2, He declares, "I HAVE HEARD THEE IN A TIME ACCEPTED." This powerful declaration signifies that God positions Himself to receive our prayers in this day of salvation. We grasp the significance of our secured place in His favor as we pray before His throne. Through Christ, we enter within the veil, standing as intercessors.

Prayer: A Pivotal Part of Coming to God in Repentance and Receiving His Grace

To be heard by God makes prayer a pivotal part of our call to approach Him in repentance, seeking His grace and mercy in times of need. He has positioned Himself to be our sufficient grace amidst our insecurities. Just as He longs for us to listen to His calling and use His wisdom and knowledge in our daily lives, He also desires to hear our voices calling out to Him in faith. The invitation to pray to the Father in Jesus' name opens the door to intimate fellowship with Him in spirit and truth. With confidence in the Spirit's assistance in prayer, we no longer fear approaching the throne of grace. Prayer is a sacred privilege granted to every believer.

Our Access to God through Christ and Escaping the Bondage of Wrong Thinking

We must never underestimate the significance of our identity in Christ, for it grants us access to God. Ephesians 2:18 affirms that through Him, we have access to the Father by one Spirit. Without Christ, we have no way of approaching God. Furthermore, I Timothy 2:5 emphasizes that there is only one mediator between God and humanity—Jesus Christ. Through Him, we have escaped the bondage of wrong thinking and the entanglements of the enemy's lies. The knowledge of our Lord and Savior, Jesus Christ, has liberated us, enabling us to walk in the truth.

The Time of Acceptance and Help in the Day of Salvation

II Corinthians 6:2 not only assures us that God has heard us, but it also declares, "AND IN THE DAY OF SALVATION HAVE I SUCCOURED THEE; behold, now is the accepted time; behold, now is the day of salvation." These powerful words from the throne of God remind us that we receive help from the Lord every day of our lives. Today is our day of salvation, and the blessings granted to us through Christ break through, penetrating our entire being as our unwavering confidence in God remains steadfast. In this belief and assurance of staying steady, God hears us, and our souls are open to the Holy Spirit. With His help, we can fully possess the promises God has made. We realize it is the Father's pleasure to bestow upon us the abundant treasures of His kingdom.

Increased Confidence and Continued Engagement in Prayer

When we obey God and fellowship with Him, our voice of faith in prayer echoes back to us as answered prayer. Knowing that God sees and comprehends all things, both seen and unseen, we can have faith when we ask Him for things according to His will. Answered prayer serves as a stimulus, fueling our confidence and encouraging us to persistently engage our hearts in prayer.

Gideon and Solomon: Examples of God's Personal Response to Prayer

Throughout the Old Testament, we witness instances where God partnered with His servants in prayer. Gideon sought an answer from God and proposed a specific request as a testament to his faith. God graciously responded by allowing dew to fall upon the fleece as Gideon had asked. Reassured by this personal demonstration of God's attentiveness, Gideon moved forward confidently, fulfilling his appointed tasks.

Another case is Solomon's prayer. He implored God to heed the cry and supplication of His servant, and the Lord appeared to Solomon by night, assuring him that He had heard his prayer. God even chose a specific place for a house of sacrifice, indicating His commitment to attending the prayers of His people. These narratives remind us that the foundation of God's house is laid in prayer and established to receive and answer prayers.

The Door of Faith and the Accepted Time

Just as God positioned Himself to answer prayers in the Old Testament when worshippers came to the temple, He places Himself to respond when we, by faith, approach Him today. When He declared to Solomon in 2 Chronicles 7:15, "Now my eyes shall be open, and mine ears attent unto the prayer *that is made* in this place." He opened the door for any voice of faith. Likewise, 2 Corinthians 6:2 presents the same door of faith for us to come boldly before the throne of grace. God's declaration, "I HAVE HEARD THEE IN A TIME ACCEPTED, AND IN THE DAY OF SALVATION HAVE I SUCCOURED THEE," resounds with power, urging us to recognize that now is the accepted time, now is the day of salvation.

May these truths resound and stir a deeper hunger for prayer. Let us confidently approach our

Heavenly Father, knowing He hears and answers our prayers according to His perfect will. May our lives be a testament to the transformative power of prayer, and may we walk in the assurance that God, our loving and attentive God, is always nearby.

Prayer

Heavenly Father: In the stillness of this moment, we humbly approach Your throne in Jesus' name. We recognize Your greatness and Your boundless love for us. We come before You with grateful hearts, knowing You hear our prayers.

Grant us the wisdom to discern Your will and the courage to walk in obedience. May Your peace encompass our lives, and Your grace sustain us through every challenge.

We surrender our desires and dreams to You, trusting You have the best plan for our lives. Align our hearts with Your purposes and fill us with Your Holy Spirit, guiding our every step.

We lift those who are hurting, in need, and searching for Your light. May Your healing touch bring comfort, Your provision meets requirements, and Your love brings hope and restoration.

Today, we seek Your face and invite Your presence to dwell within us. Mold us into vessels of love, compassion, and grace, reflecting Your character to our world.

Thank You, Heavenly Father, for the privilege of prayer. We rejoice in the assurance that You hear us

and eagerly anticipate the miracles You will perform. All glory and honor belong to You, now and forever.
In Jesus' name, Amen.

Chapter Thirteen:
From Midnight to Morning

"And at midnight Paul and Silas prayed, and sang praises unto God: and the prisoners heard them."
(Acts 16:25)

Midnight of Worship:

A Paul and Silas, filled with unwavering confidence in God, praised and worshiped Him even in the darkest hour of their lives. Their worship and praise resonated with the Father, causing an earthquake that shook the prison doors and changed their circumstances. Despite being held captive, they did not cease to worship God. Their worship became a powerful manifestation of God's presence and His ability to deliver them. Even their fellow prisoners' unregenerate minds could not hinder the flow of their worship. Their praise shattered the chains that bound them. Recognizing God's sovereignty in every situation brings about transformation. Regardless of the accusations against believers, God's presence is always available for deliverance.

A Witness to Salvation:

The Father heard Paul and Silas' voices, and the prisoners around them also listened to their worship. Their praise of God while in captivity brought about the salvation of the jailer, the one responsible for keeping them bound. Paul and Silas were undeterred by the physical chains that held them captive. Their strength rested in the knowledge that God could deliver them. Their minds remained free to pray and praise God. Salvation was visibly on display within the prison walls. The power of God openly demonstrated deliverance from the hands of men.

The Mindset of Christ:

The presence of the mind of Christ within Paul and Silas prevented them from being defeated. Their focus was on praising God while He worked out their situation. They were not worried because they knew God had the power to deliver them. Their worship led to the opening of prison doors for all the prisoners. The earthquake, a manifestation of God's presence, shook the jail and loosed the prison doors.

A Testimony for Others:

When we walk through difficult circumstances, our praise allows others to witness the glory of God in ways they may not have experienced before. Paul and

Silas allowed God's glory within them to overflow through singing and prayer, reflecting the image of Christ.

Divine Purpose in Worship:

The manifestation of God's presence, responding to the pure worship emanating from the hearts of Paul and Silas, served a greater purpose beyond their worship. It displayed God's glory amidst human ignorance, bringing deliverance to His faithful servants. The magistrates thought they could suppress the spread of the Gospel by imprisoning them, but God chose an earthquake to demonstrate that human authority cannot hinder His plans. The deliverance extended to Paul and Silas and the jailer's household, leading to their salvation. Paul and Silas trusted God and allowed Him to fight their battle at midnight.

From Midnight to Morning:

Any form of bondage or captivity must yield when we remain steadfast in God and refuse to give up. Scripture reminds us in Psalm 30:5 that "...weeping may endure for a night, but joy cometh in the morning." There is always a moment when God turns our darkest hour into a new day. When we trust Him, He gives us the strength to face adversity, just as He did for Paul and Silas. Their dedication to God's work for the salvation of humanity culminated in signs and wonders within the prison that held them captive.

Prayer

Heavenly Father, we seek Your presence and power during our darkest hours. Just as Paul and Silas prayed and praised You at midnight, we come before You with hearts full of gratitude and faith. We believe that You hear us when we call upon Your name.

Let our worship be a beacon of light during darkness, a testimony that draws others closer to You. May our praise break every chain that seeks to bind us, for You alone have the power to free us. We surrender our burdens and challenges to You, knowing You are more significant than any circumstance we face. Your love and mercy transcend all limitations, and Your deliverance knows no bounds.

As we lift our voices in prayer, we trust that You will work miracles in our lives. May Your presence manifest suddenly, shaking the foundations of our trials and ushering in a new morning of joy and victory. We declare that we are more than conquerors through Christ who strengthens us. Grant us the mindset of Christ, unwavering in our trust and praise, knowing that You are fighting our battles on our behalf.

Thank You, Father, for hearing our prayers and the assurance that You are with us every step of the way. We surrender ourselves to Your will and invite Your kingdom to reign.

In Jesus' name. Amen.

Chapter Fourteen
The Mantle of Prayer

James 5:16 declares, "The effectual fervent prayer of a righteous man availeth much."

Prayer is a powerful tool bestowed upon us, enabling us to draw near God and experience His grace. Through prayer, we can exercise dominion on the earth and break free from the chains that once held us captive.

Prayer encompasses the highest aim of the Father's name, kingdom, and will. Jesus taught us to pray the Lord's Prayer, revealing the hidden glory from hallowing His name. As we enter the fullness of God in Christ, we are free from the bondage of sin, thereby entering the realm of prayer.

Elijah, known as a man of prayer, sought to hallow God's name among the children of Israel through his intercession. After a prolonged drought, his effectual prayer brought about a revival in the people's hearts. They proclaimed in 1 Kings 18:39, "The LORD, he is the God; the LORD, he is the God." Elijah's prayer ignited a change in the darkness that had enveloped their hearts, liberating them from the captivity of pagan worship.

Throughout the scriptures, we find numerous examples of persistence in prayer. In Genesis 32:24-26, Jacob wrestled with an angel until daybreak, refusing to let go until he received a blessing. Similarly, we must display unwavering resolve in our prayer life, clinging to God for His blessings.

Abraham's intercession for the righteous in Sodom and Gomorrah displayed a zealous heart that drew near to God. He pleaded with the Lord not to destroy the righteous alongside the wicked, communing with God until his intercession prevailed. We, too, should exhibit such zeal and persistence in our prayers.

Luke 18:1 reminds us to pray continually and not grow weary. Let us not lose heart in doing good but instead persevere in prayer, relying on the Lord's promised provision. A vibrant prayer life is indispensable for every believer.

Prayer holds within it the power of transition. Through effective and fervent praying, we are transformed from glory to glory, from the midst of conflict to the triumph of conquest. In prayer, we find rest and victory in Christ, who manifests His life and faith within us. Our faith in the Son of God is the victory that overcomes the world. Therefore, let us press on and continue to pray with unwavering faith.

Prayer

Heavenly Father, we come before You with grateful hearts, acknowledging the power and significance of prayer in our lives. We thank You for the privilege to draw near to You and experience Your grace and presence.

Today, we surrender ourselves to Your divine will and purpose. We ask for the mantle of prayer to rest upon us, empowering us to pray effectually and fervently. May our prayers avail much and bring about transformation in our lives and the lives of others.

Help us to hallow Your name and advance Your kingdom through our prayers. Strengthen our resolve to pray, just as Jacob wrestled with the angel until he received a blessing. Grant us a zealous heart like Abraham, who interceded for the righteous in Sodom and Gomorrah.

Lord, we refuse to grow weary in prayer. We commit to praying without ceasing and not fainting, knowing that You are faithful to hear and answer our petitions. We embrace the power of prayer as a means of transition and victory, enabling us to go from glory to glory in our worship and conquer the challenges we face.

Thank You for the assurance that You hear our prayers and that they have a significant impact. We trust You and rely on Your provision and guidance in all things.

In Jesus' mighty name. Amen.

Chapter Fifteen:
Alive Unto God

J ust beneath the surface of our thought life is the witness of the Holy Spirit. He calls to the deep within us to rise and begin living in the things already ordered and ordained for our life in Christ. By embracing His presence, we unite with the purposes and blessings God has prepared for those who love Him.

Born into God's Family

Through accepting Jesus Christ as our Savior, each believer becomes alive unto God. We are born into the family of God through Christ, called to be lively stones, a spiritual house, and a holy and royal priesthood in this generation. We are chosen to show God's praises and live separated unto Him for His glory and purpose.

The Church as the Pillar of Truth

We serve as the pillar and ground of truth in the Church of the living God. Through the resurrection power of Jesus Christ, we are alive unto God. As we genuinely embrace this reality, our fellowship with Him deepens, and we can partake more freely of our daily inheritance in Christ.

Embracing God's Plan and Purpose

We should be grateful for the rich life God has given us in His plan and purpose through Christ. Our salvation includes a high calling and inheritance, and it is essential not to walk beneath that privilege. Let us turn inward and examine if we have lost sight of the reality of our spiritual being. We should no longer neglect claiming our daily inheritance but re-think the value of being called unto glory and virtue in the Kingdom of God.

Worshiping God in Spirit and Truth

In our faith journey, we must learn to face life and worship God in spirit and truth, fully possessing all He has fulfilled for us in Christ. True worship brings us into the heart of God's purpose for our lives. By acknowledging that we are alive unto God, we can access His inheritance through the riches of His glory, making our riches in Christ known. We must live in the exalted position of being alive unto God in Christ.

Walking in Authority and Diligently Seeking God

Every believer sanctified in Christ Jesus has a sphere of influence where they daily participate in God's plan through acts of obedience. Since we possess authority over the enemy and his devices from the position of being in Christ, it is God's will that we walk in the delegated authority each day. Our devotion to attain our salvation daily stands manifested through our trust in Him. Diligently seeking God is rewarded, as He is a rewarder of those who diligently seek Him.

Avoiding Captivity and Walking by Faith

The challenge for every believer is to avoid captivity by obediently following what God has ordered and ordained for our lives on earth. Walking in the newness of life in Christ requires us to walk by faith, not sight. With the Bible as our lamp of truth, we can rely on the wisdom and experiences of others who have discovered the treasure of Christ within.

Unveiling the Heart of Christ

Let us submit to God's thoughts and ways so that we stand before Him in agreement. A pure heart is free from falsehood, sustained by the thoughts of God's Spirit in living out our lives before Him. Allow the word of God to expose any flaws causing captivity and examine the impact of such captivity, resolving within ourselves that enough is enough.

Becoming a Living Witness

The story of the Samaritan woman's testimony in John Chapter 4 exemplifies how encountering Jesus can break the chains of darkness and prejudice. Her transformation from a woman burdened by her past to a living witness impacted those around her. In the same way, our lives become open letters read by the world, reflecting the heart of Christ within us. We are no longer captives to darkness but alive unto God with purpose and vision. Be awakened to your identity in Christ daily.

Decreeing Freedom and Embracing Identity in Christ

Let us consider and remember how God sees us and how the mind of Christ enables us to bring forth a Christ-centered life that touches others. An inward transformation creates an inward experience with the Lord. We no longer see outward appearances or family traditions, which make bondage, as the way to please God. Instead, we stand in our new identity, alive unto God in Christ. It is an "of Him, through Him, and to Him" relationship that reflects God's glory and is worthy of our declaration and decree.

Rewriting the Next Chapter and Taking a Stance

As we contemplate rewriting the next chapter of our lives, make it legible and robust through our identity in Christ. May others see the excellent work of God in our hearts as we take a stance against an impoverished mentality that accepts things as they are. We declare that we have rule over our spirit, protecting our lives from the enemy's invasion. Bound by nothing, we stand firm in our new identity, alive unto God, and bring glory to His name.

Released from the Bondage of External Appearances

In the past, I found myself trapped in the belief that my outward appearance was crucial to how others perceived me. Adorned in religious attire, I sought validation through external measures, yet my inner self remained unfulfilled. It was a state of captivity, unaware of the transformation that awaited me. Being told that I needed to wear white clothing to identify me as saved threw me into a pseudo-operation of religion instead of an inward relationship with the Lord.

Delivered into Inner Transformation

In His boundless grace, the Lord intervened and liberated me from the bondage of external appearances. He saw beyond the façade and

145

recognized the longing within my heart. Through His divine intervention, He initiated a profound inner transformation that transcended the confines of external adornment.

The Quest for the Holy Spirit

During those times, teachings emphasized the connection between outward appearance and the reception of the Holy Spirit. In my earnest pursuit of a more profound encounter with God, I diligently approached the altar, seeking the Holy Spirit with a genuine expectation to speak in tongues as evidence of His indwelling presence.

A Sacred Encounter and Prophetic Words

One momentous night, as I stood at the altar, the presence of God manifested before me, appearing as "a wheel in the middle of a wheel." In that sacred moment, the Holy Spirit spoke directly to the depths of my being, revealing a profound truth: "The way over to the other side is to trust and obey." It was a divine declaration that brought instant peace and understanding, solidifying the knowledge that the Holy Spirit was alive within me. In that revelation, I fully realized I was alive unto God.

Stepping Forward in Trust and Obedience

Empowered by the words spoken by the Holy Spirit, I embarked on a journey of wholehearted trust and obedience. The transformative encounter at the altar propelled me forward, igniting a newfound faith and deepening my dependence on God's guidance. It was a step into a realm of divine empowerment and an awakening to the reality of the Holy Spirit's work in my life.

Promptings of Spiritual Gifts

As I continued to walk in obedience and surrender, the Holy Spirit continued to renew and equip me with various spiritual gifts. These promptings were tangible manifestations of His presence and an expression of His desire to work through me for His divine purposes. Each prompting served as a reminder that I was alive unto God, entrusted with the privilege of partnering with Him in His kingdom work.

These sections in this chapter recount the journey from captivity in external appearances to a profound transformation within, highlighting the quest for the Holy Spirit and the subsequent encounter that solidified the reality of being alive unto God. It concludes with the renewal and prompting of spiritual gifts that continue to shape and empower my spiritual journey.

Now, as you contemplate rewriting the next chapter of your life, in the process of breaking free from captivity, allow your identity in Christ to shine forth so that others may witness the incredible work of God in your heart. Take a bold stance and declare that you will not allow confinement to an impoverished mentality that accepts things as they are. Remember the wisdom of Proverbs 25:28, which warns that a person without self-control is like a city with broken walls, vulnerable to enemy invasion. Declare that you stand freed from familial traditions or practices that may create bondage in your new life in Christ. Embrace your unique identity and stand as one alive unto God in Christ. He is the Lord of your identity, and through your identity, He reveals His lordship. It is a profound relationship with God—an "of Him, through Him, and to Him" a connection we have in Christ. This identity matches God's bio in Romans 11:36: "For of him and through him, and to him, are all things: to whom be glory forever. Amen."

Prayer

Heavenly Father, we come before You with hearts filled with gratitude and a desire to embrace the truth of being alive unto You. Thank You for the revelation in Your Word that our old selves have been crucified with Christ, and through Him, we stand freed from sin and alive unto You.

Holy Father, we invite You to stir the deep places within us, awakening us to the abundant life You have prepared for us in Christ. Help us to fully comprehend and embrace the reality of being born into Your family as lively stones, a holy and royal priesthood. May we shine forth Your praises and fulfill Your purpose in this generation.

Lord, we acknowledge that Your Church is the pillar and ground of truth and gladly accept we are part of it. Enable us to walk in the resurrection power of Jesus Christ, deepening our fellowship with You and experiencing the fullness of our inheritance in Him.

We repent for moments when we have failed to grasp the richness of life given to us in Christ. Help us to realign our thoughts and perspectives, recognizing the high calling we have received and the privilege of being alive unto You. Let us no longer walk beneath our true identity but rise in faith, embracing the reality of who we are in Christ.

Father, we surrender to Your thoughts and ways, knowing that a pure heart aligns with Your truth. Expose any areas of captivity in our lives and empower us to break free from them. We desire to live in the newness of life, walking by faith and not by sight.

As we reflect on the transformation of the Samaritan woman in John 4, we ask that You break every chain of darkness and prejudice in our lives. Like her, may our encounter with Jesus lead to a thirst for more of His prophetic utterances and a testimony that impacts those around us.

Lord, help us to live as open letters read by the world, revealing the heart of Christ in us. Give us the wisdom to walk in our sphere of influence, exercising the authority You have given us over the enemy. Teach us to diligently seek You, knowing that You reward those who earnestly seek You.

We declare that we are no longer captives of anything that hinders our walk with You. With faith and trust, we step into the fullness of our identity in Christ and embrace the victory You have already prepared for us.

In Jesus' name. Amen.

A Prayer Covering

Dear Heavenly Father, I acknowledge the greatness of Your name and the power that You possess. Your Word reminds us of the consequences of rejecting Christ and avoiding Your divine voice. Help us, O Lord, to grasp the weight of this truth and its spiritual implications.

Since the very foundation of the world, You have set forth the path of redemption for humanity through Your beloved Son, Jesus Christ. In Your perfect counsel, You designed a plan to make us whole, complete, and united in Christ, the very One through whom You created all things. The fellowship of this mystery, hidden in You from the beginning, has now been revealed through Your Son.

I understand that rejecting Christ leads to captivity and invites Your judgment. Your Word declares that those who reject Him and His teachings will face judgment on the last day. How fearful it is to turn away from Jesus Christ who offers salvation and eternal life.

Help me, Lord, to understand our identity in Christ. May this revelation set us apart from the deception and lies of the enemy. Enable us to grasp Christ's victory over the enemy, an accomplishment we can experience daily. I refuse to deny Your intended victory for my life, for it is through Christ's sacrifice that I have been set free from guilt and given the gift of righteousness.

I firmly establish that Your Word, the Bible, is our life's inspired and profitable guide. Through Your breath, the Scriptures teach us about Christ and His redemptive work for humanity. It is the source of light and truth, unveiling the mysteries of our existence on Earth. You have made Yourself believable and approachable by creating us in Your image, impregnated with the capacity to will, conceive, and believe.

Precious Father, no matter what others may say or how they may reject it, Your Word remains valid, accurate, and sound. Man's dismissal of the proof of Your existence in creation damages his conscience and hampers his reasoning ability. May we not disregard this undeniable evidence but embrace it wholeheartedly.

Lord, the rejection of Christ and His redemptive work leads us into the captivity of lies and false teachings devised by the devil. Your Word is the antidote to these deceptions, offering us the wisdom, knowledge, and understanding our souls crave. Grant us the grace to accept and acknowledge that Your Word is inspired and faithful to our deepest needs.

In this day of grace, Holy Father, help us stay persuaded with the assurance of understanding Your knowledge. May we fully grasp the mystery of God, the Father, and Christ, for in the Godhead are hidden all the treasures of wisdom and knowledge. I recognize that You have deposited this treasure in our fragile earthen vessels, revealing Your abundant grace, love, and mercy. Let us never underestimate the value of this treasure within us, for it is the key to our freedom.

Just as Apostle Paul desired for the saints and faithful brethren in Christ to be comforted, knitted together in love, and fully assured of understanding, we want the same. May we acknowledge the mystery of God, the Father, and Christ, realizing that all wisdom and knowledge reside in Him. This treasure within us overflows with Your grace, love, and mercy.

Lord, please grant repentance and acknowledgment of the truth to those who oppose themselves. Rescue them from the devil's snare: ignorance of Your will leads to captivity. May we never be ignorant of Satan's devices, but rather, equip ourselves with Your truth and walk in the freedom that only comes through knowing You.

As Jesus declared to His followers, let us know the truth that sets us free. By walking with Him truthfully, we become His disciples, partaking in the freedom He offers. Thank You for the Son who makes us truly free.

Father, as your children, we live delivered through knowing the truth rather than in the bondage of ignorance. Your Word brings healing and comfort to troubled souls. May wisdom and knowledge enter our hearts, becoming pleasant to our souls. Through discretion and understanding, preserve and keep us, O Lord.

As we submit ourselves to Your Word, may it enter our souls as a shining light, preserving us from stumbling. May Your words bring understanding to the simple and illuminate our minds in the face of Jesus Christ, the embodiment of truth. We heed Your call to step out of the darkness of sin's captivity into the glorious liberty of being Your sons and daughters through Jesus Christ, our Savior. In Jesus' name, I honor, praise, and worship You, Heavenly Father. Amen.

About
Dr. Christine M. Hubbard

From welfare struggles as a divorcee with four children, the hand of the Lord carved an extraordinary path through her faith journey. She was part of the welfare system and public housing for twelve years with four children. Remarkably, all her children obtained four-year college degrees during this time. Rising above personal adversities, in 2010, she earned a Doctoral Degree in Theology. She is now President of GAP Ministries College of Theology and founder of GAP Ministries Community Church. Her story embodies resilience, determination and stands as a beacon of inspiration, proving that one's origin does not dictate their destination.